THE FOUNDATIONS OF MORALITY

Unwin Education Books

Education Since 1800 IVOR MORRISH
Physical Education for Teaching BARBARA CHURCHER
Organising and Integrating the First School Day JOY TAYLOR
The Philosophy of Education: An Introduction HARRY SCHOFIELD
Assessment and Testing: An Introduction HARRY SCHOFIELD
Education: Its Nature and Purpose M. V. C. JEFFREYS
Learning in the Primary School KENNETH HASLAM
The Sociology of Education: An Introduction IVOR MORRISH
Developing a Curriculum AUDREY and HOWARD NICHOLLS
Teacher Education and Cultural Change H. DUDLEY PLUNKETT and
  JAMES LYNCH
Reading and Writing in the First School JOY TAYLOR
Approaches to Drama DAVID A. MALE
Aspects of Learning BRIAN O'CONNELL
Focus on Meaning JOAN TOUGH
Moral Education WILLIAM KAY
Concepts in Primary Education JOHN E. SADLER
Moral Philosophy for Education ROBIN BARROW
Principles of Classroom Learning and Perception RICHARD J. MUELLER
Education and the Community ERIC MIDWINTER
Creative Teaching AUDREY and HOWARD NICHOLLS
The Preachers of Culture MARGARET MATHIESON
Mental Handicap: An Introduction DAVID EDEN
Aspects of Educational Change IVOR MORRISH
Beyond Initial Reading JOHN POTTS
The Foundation of Maths in the Infant School JOY TAYLOR
Common Sense and the Curriculum ROBIN BARROW
The Second 'R' WILLIAM HARPIN
The Diploma Disease RONALD DORE
The Development of Meaning JOAN TOUGH
The Place of Commonsense in Educational Thought LIONEL ELVIN
Language in Teaching and Learning HAZEL FRANCIS
Patterns of Education in the British Isles NIGEL GRANT and ROBERT BELL
Philosophical Foundations for the Curriculum ALLEN BRENT
World Faiths in Education W. OWEN COLE
Classroom Language: What Sort? JILL RICHARDS
Philosophy and Human Movement DAVID BEST
Secondary Schools and the Welfare Network DAPHNE JOHNSON *et al.*
Educating Adolescent Girls E. M. CHANDLER
Classroom Observation of Primary School Children RICHARD W. MILLS
Essays on Educators R. S. PETERS
Comparative Education: Some Considerations of Method BRIAN HOLMES
Education and the Individual BRENDA COHEN
Moral Development and Moral Education R. S. PETERS
In-Service Education within the School ROLAND W. MORANT
Learning to Read HAZEL FRANCIS
Children and Schooling PHILIP GAMMAGE
Relating to Learning PETER KUTNICK
The Foundations of Morality JOEL J. KUPPERMAN

The Foundations of Morality

JOEL J. KUPPERMAN
The University of Connecticut

London
GEORGE ALLEN & UNWIN
Boston   Sydney

George Allen & Unwin (Publishers) Ltd,
40 Museum Street, London WC1A 1LU, UK

George Allen & Unwin (Publishers) Ltd,
Park Lane, Hemel Hempstead, Herts HP2 4TE, UK

Allen & Unwin, Inc.,
9 Winchester Terrace, Winchester, Mass. 01890, USA

George Allen & Unwin Australia Pty Ltd,
8 Napier Street, North Sydney, NSW 2060, Australia

First published in 1983

British Library Cataloguing in Publication Data

Kupperman, Joel J.
  The foundations of morality.—(Unwin education
books)
1. Ethics
BJ1012   170
ISBN 0-04-370124-8

Library of Congress Cataloging in Publication Data

Kupperman, Joel.
  The foundations of morality.

(Unwin education books)
Includes index.
1. Ethics.   I. Title.   II. Series.
BJ1012.K83   1983   170   82-13879
ISBN 0-04-370125-6 (pbk.)

Typeset in 10 on 12 Times by Inforum Ltd, Portsmouth
Printed in Great Britain by Biddles Ltd, Guildford, Surrey

Contents

Preface   *page* ix

Part One   Morality as We Know It   1

  1   Morality as a System of Strong Demands   3
  2   Morality as Law   18
  3   Morality as Interpersonally Neutral   34

Part Two   The Need for Ethical Theory   47

  4   The Nature of Ethical Theory   49
  5   Difficult Cases and Moral Progress   58
  6   Utilitarianism and Value   69

Part Three   The Case for Consequentialism   91

  7   First Pattern of Argument   93
  8   Second Pattern of Argument   112
  9   Third Pattern of Argument   121

Part Four   Humanising Ethics   131

 10   The Gap between What Would Be for the Best and What
      We Should Do   133
 11   The Role of Self-Interest and Personal Relations   142
 12   Ethical Education   150

Index   161

Preface

To say that morality has foundations is to say that it can be unified, made sense of, and modified by ethical theory. Morality does not have foundations in the way in which an axiomatic system has its axioms as a foundation, nor is it true that people in general base their morality on ethical theory. Common-sense morality can survive without a foundation of ethical theory; but I argue that it cannot begin to solve all its problems, and without a foundation it may appear as a set of arbitrary dogmas. This work extends the thesis of my earlier book, *Ethical Knowledge*, by not only arguing that ethics is 'cognitive' but also exploring the kinds of ethical knowledge and the ways in which ethical claims can be challenged and justified.

The Foundations of Morality was completed in 1981 during tenure of a twelve months' fellowship for independent study and research given by the National Endowment for the Humanities. I am grateful to the Master (Professor Alan Heimert) and members of Eliot House, Harvard, for their hospitality during the spring semester of 1981. Lynn Paine, Joel Marks, and Larry May each read some chapters of the manuscript, and curbed some of my excesses. Marie Becker and Carol Leary (who typed the final versions) provided invaluable assistance. My greatest debt remains to Karen Ordahl Kupperman, from whose energy and good sense I have benefited.

Part One

Morality as We Know It

Chapter 1

Morality as a System of Strong Demands

Morality tells us, and others, what ought and ought not to be done. Because moral judgements can be applied both to ourselves and to other people, morality can seem to have two countenances. Both are stern. One is the countenance of strict demands on oneself. Morality can keep us up to standard, but it also can tell us that our behaviour is not good enough. This countenance of morality has close links with guilt: indeed, it may be questioned whether a feeling of regret can be called guilt unless it is associated with a negative moral judgement of some past conduct on one's part.

The other countenance of morality is outward-directed censoriousness. To consider someone immoral is a special way of looking down on that person. It can bring great pressure, and is frequently coupled with a desire to harm. John Stuart Mill asserted that a sense that those making wrong choices should be punished defined the realm of the moral. We judge people to be immoral only if they are not conforming to our standards, and in this respect moral judgement can be viewed as a special form of pressure on those who do not conform. This was Nietzsche's view; and it is one of the reasons why, although he felt free to make value judgements of various sorts, he was opposed to morality. Few people would go as far as Nietzsche in opposing morality. But one of the differences between Western culture in the late twentieth century and Western culture in the nineteenth century appears to be that moral judgements are now made less frequently, often with less pressure, and about a somewhat narrower range of subjects, than had been the case. As we shall see, morality appears to be gaining territory in some areas while losing it in others; but the over-all trend is towards diminution. Someone who makes moral judgements too frequently, about too wide a range of subjects, is said to be 'moralistic'; and in this sense we consider that some of our ancestors were a shade moralistic.

Might morality entirely disappear? Like any other human device, it would disappear if it were totally ineffective. One could imagine a world in which no one listened to moral advice or censure, and transgressors just laughed at moral judgements. Our world on some occasions may seem uncomfortably like that; but most of the time morality does have its influence, and transgressors cannot entirely ignore moral judgements. It is difficult to believe that this will drastically change in the foreseeable future. Whatever the shape and boundaries may be of the morality taught a few hundred years from now, we can assume that there will be a morality.

Morality would also disappear if it were not needed. Kant claimed that beings of a holy will, who automatically choose what is right, would not need the constraint of morality. Clearly he was right. Moral judgements presuppose that it is conceivable that one might do the wrong thing, so that the moral judgement tells or reminds us what is right. We do not need a set of judgements telling us to breathe. Some people have believed that in an ideal society humanity might attain a good-hearted innocence that would eliminate the need for morality. This, however, seems to be an excessively romantic view of human possibilities. Even Lenin believed that in the ideal society, when the state withered away, moral judgements within the community would take the place of the state. To believe that in an ideal society morality would not be necessary is to blame all man's ills on existing societies, and to ignore the fact that these societies are all human creations. If original sin means that humanity has always the capacity for evil, then we must affirm original sin.

To say that morality will always be needed is to take one step towards explaining why it originally was needed. Moral judgements and concepts, of course, are creations of human thought (although it seems highly likely that other intelligent beings would create something similar). They must have been created for a reason, and associated with that must be a function that they fulfil.

Thomas Hobbes claimed that both morality and the apparatus of the state arose out of a need for protection. It is as if, he said, our ancestors had signed a social contract, giving up certain liberties in return for security. The alternative would be a state of nature, in which life would be nasty, brutish, and short. The protection that morality and the state provide is not absolute. There still are immoral people, and illegal acts are performed, sometimes without being punished. But morality cannot function unless the majority of people behave morally most of the time, and something similar is true for our system of justice. We need locks on our doors, and we may have to be cautious in certain situations; but we are much more secure than we would be in a state of nature.

On such a view the core of morality must be injunctions against harming others. It is because morality forbids murder, theft, torture, etc., that it promotes our security. Indeed, it is worth reminding ourselves that injunctions of this sort have played a central role in our moral tradition, going back to the Ten Commandments. We need the reminder because morality, like so many other products of human thought, has both a core and a periphery; and the periphery can sometimes engross our attention.

It is still true that many people, when they hear of morality, think first of sex. This is so true that many people who oppose traditional sexual morality will speak derisively of morality, while making it clear that they have the strongest negative feelings of a moral sort about murder, torture, etc. Plainly there is some confusion here about what morality is. The confusion is promoted by two facts. One is that, while judgements about sexual practices were not at the core of traditional morality, they have been promoted with especial zealousness, in that the temptations to break these rules are stronger and more recurrent, for most people, than are temptations to break other rules of traditional morality. The second fact is that judgements about rightness, wrongness, or tolerability of various sexual practices are now in a conceptual no-man's-land. Many people now would no longer regard them as moral judgements, for reasons which we shall later explain. Some people, of course, still consider them moral judgements; and this makes them, as territory being fought over, seem especially important.

In any event, we can follow Hobbes to the extent of saying that the core of traditional morality consisted of rules (against murder, theft, etc.) designed to prevent harm. Some contemporary philosophers have argued that there is a very close conceptual link between morality and harm. On this view, certain practices (for example a man's clasping his hands three times an hour while turning north-north-west) could not be made the subjects of moral judgement unless in some odd way it was thought that the practices either brought about or prevented harm. Presumably, on this view, rules governing sexual practices found a place in traditional morality only because it was judged that they prevented harm: either direct harm to individuals, or harm to the social fabric.

There is much to be said for this view, and indeed my judgement is that we could not encounter anything that we would call a morality (say in a primitive tribe, or among beings from another planet) that did not assign a central role to rules forbidding harm. But it is not clear that everything contained in traditional morality can be accounted for in this way. It may be that some practices have been condemned primarily because they were thought of as disgusting. This condemnation might have been rationalised by the additional charge that they were in some subtle way harmful to the person engaging in them; but strictly speaking there is no logical contradiction in describing a practice as disgusting but not harmful, and as disgusting in such a peculiar way as to be immoral. Some people are more prone to view a practice as disgusting if it seems to give great pleasure to those who engage in it, and if clasping one's hands three times an hour while turning north-north-west generally produced sexual ecstasy it might be treated by some as a stronger candidate for moral judgement. Whether an entire morality can have as its core condemnation of practices of this sort is another question. Such a system of condemnation would be so very different from any morality with which we are acquainted that I judge we would have to find another word for it.

The question naturally arises: if a system of condemnation is not a morality, then what can it be? In our culture there are a few main alternatives; other cultures might develop alternatives undreamed of by us. We have a system of condemnation taught to us as children, in terms of criteria for good manners. Thus someone can be uncouth, rude, or more generally a slob, without being immoral. To be a slob, of course, is to fail in more than one department of behaviour: the judgement suggests aesthetic failings as well as bad manners. Our aesthetic system of condemnation perhaps has its primary use in relation to works of art and scenes in nature, which can be ugly, inelegant, confused, or boring; but people too are sometimes termed ugly, repulsive, or tasteless. We have a system of condemnation for conduct in practical matters, too. It is not clear why it should matter to us that someone is competent, unless we depend directly on that person; but we do make negative judgements of people who are incompetent or impractical. Terms like 'ineffectual' and 'loser' testify to our concern in this area. Someone who thinks that morality counts for everything in Western culture should reflect on the fact that someone can be a repulsive slob and a loser and yet never do anything morally wrong.

Morality, aesthetics, manners, and practical prudence are of course not just systems of condemnation. They tell us what to do, and can be used by us in helping others decide what to do. This is in fact the main role of practical prudence; and, even in the cases of morality and manners, it would be wrong to regard them too exclusively as defending against bad conduct. Morality and manners have their positive aspects, and with any case of someone who is condemned by them we can juxtapose a much larger number of cases of people who are enabled to sort out what is expected of them, perform this while avoiding transgressions, and go about their business unscathed.

Judgements that imply guidance, to oneself and to others, have been termed by R.M. Hare 'prescriptive'. Moral, aesthetic, and practical judgements, and judgements concerning manners, are in normal contexts prescriptive judgements. One has to introduce the phrase 'normal contexts' because there are groups of people and situations for which characterising something as immoral, rude, ugly, boring, or practically ruinous would provoke laughter or indifference. The pop artist who praised a work of art as boring, saying 'I love to be bored', has his counterpart in relation to morality and other prescriptive systems. What is interesting in his remarks is not only that they can be made but the air of paradox that remains with them. A similar air of paradox surrounds Satan's (in Milton's *Paradise Lost*) saying 'Evil be thou my good', even though we know perfectly well what he means.

In very many contexts moral, aesthetic and practical judgements, and judgements of manners, are treated as positive guidance. But not only is this so, it must be so. That is, the point – the meaning – of these judgements is to function as guidance; and even someone who decided to reject or ignore such a judgement would not understand what it meant unless he or she realised that it had built into it that function. To use an analogy: knives can be used for a number of things besides cutting, but if this were not their normal use they would not be knives. Similarly, the use, that is to say the meaning, of a favourable moral judgement is to commend. Thus Hare is right about prescriptivity. But we must say that there are a number of types of prescriptive judgements, and moral judgements are only one of them.

How then do we distinguish moral judgements from other types of prescriptive judgement? What determines our classification? Before we approach this, we should realise that it is peculiarly a modern Western problem. In the classics of Chinese ethics there is no concept closely corresponding to our concept 'moral', and thus no sharp distinction made between moral judgements and other forms of advice as to how life should be led. It is questionable also whether there is any such distinction in ancient Greek philosophy. We might judge, for example, that Aristotle's praise of the contemplative life as the best kind of life lies outside morality, in that no one today who agrees with Aristotle is likely to judge a person immoral simply for choosing some other kind of life. But it is far from clear that Aristotle would have made the distinction that this implies. We can also say, correctly, that Confucian philosophers viewed filial impiety much as we view acts that we consider immoral. The ancient Greek and Chinese philosophers (with some exceptions) were prepared to make what *we* would term moral judgements. What is absent is not morality (or at least something very like it) but rather the special concept of morality.

Thus, while great philosophers have written about the division between morality and the rest of life, they are all modern Western philosophers, in accordance with our preoccupation with the special features of morality. Immanuel Kant, for example, distinguished between the categorical imperative, which is not goal-directed at all, and hypothetical imperatives, which tell us how to achieve either particular goals or the general goal of happiness. Kant's claim is that only an imperative that is not goal-directed qualifies as moral. Implicit in this also is the claim that much of Greek ethical philosophy, which tells us how to achieve well-being in our lives, does not qualify as morality. Only acts done out of duty, rather than from an inclination directed towards some goal, can qualify as moral.

Kant's view of what constitutes morality contains a rich mixture of claims and assumptions; and, although the rococo brilliance of Kant's edifice notoriously resists analysis, we should pause for some attempt to separate elements. Kant answers, in a related way, the following questions: (1) What counts as a moral problem?, (2) Under what circumstances should someone get moral credit for a decision?, and (3) How do we derive criteria for testing whether a moral decision is correct? The distinction between hypothetical imperatives and the categorical imperative gives his answer to (1), but it also plays a part in the answers to (2) and (3). If a decision is made on the basis of inclination towards a goal (which a hypothetical imperative tells one how to achieve), rather than from a sense of duty (respect for the deliverances of the categorical imperative), it gets no moral credit. Thus the answer to (2) is that someone gets moral credit for a decision if and only if it is one which should be approached purely in terms of the categorical imperative, and he or she does approach the decision purely in terms of the categorical imperative, rather than being influenced by hypothetical imperatives. The answer to (3) also consists of the categorical imperative. One reason why hypothetical imperatives are irrelevant to the testing of a moral decision is that the consequences of an action always require empirical determination, and (because of his initial assumption that morality must be universal and objective) Kant requires that the testing of a moral decision be *a priori* rather than empirical.

It has to be said right at the start that there is considerable plausibility in all of Kant's answers. We do not normally consider problems of how to achieve such-and-such to be moral problems. Even the problem of how to achieve the greatest human happiness, each person counting for one, is (put that way) a technical problem, one of planning, rather than a moral problem. Thus there clearly is some truth to Kant's answer to (1). His answer to (2) offends many people nowadays. It seems austere: why should we not give moral credit to acts performed out of love or kindness? Why should only dry hearts and pursed lips be allowed moral credit? But if we clear our minds of cant, we find that Kant has captured a good deal of what our cultural tradition has restricted morality to be. The reader should reflect that a man who because of principle saves a drowning person he dislikes, in a situation in which there is no hope of a reward, would be spoken of as acting morally; if he saved a person he loved most in the world, we would praise him in other terms. Morality is just one system of judgement, and impulses of love and kindness get high marks in other categories. Finally there is this much plausibility to Kant's answer to (3): our cultural tradition has forged close links between morality and principle, and it is widely assumed that moral principles can be applied *a priori* to a case once we have a clear vision of the features of the case.

Words like 'duty' had a special resonance in Kant's day that they perhaps no longer possess, but we still speak with especial moral approval of 'women (or men) of principle'.

Kant's answer to (3) can best be discussed in the next two chapters, which contain a lengthy discussion of moral rules and principles. Let me briefly say that Kant's answer to (2), judged in relation to our current distinction between moral approbation and other forms of approbation, appears half true. It is true that we do not normally give moral credit for acts that grow immediately and naturally out of impulses of love or kindness. We normally do not accord parents who love their children moral praise for being loving parents (although we would assign moral blame if they neglected their children in a clear-cut and dramatic way). On the other hand, we do praise people morally for actions that involve difficulty in decision, and that are decided upon finally because of amiability or kindness. A woman who hesitates to give money to a beggar, feeling that she needs the money herself, but who finally gives out of a sense of kindness would be generally considered to have done something morally virtuous. We generally praise people morally who, out of general benevolence, make an effort to help others. Perhaps the key distinction here is not Kant's, between duty and inclination, but rather between effortless acts and those that involve effort, hesitation or difficulty in decision. We must remember that morality, with its apparatus of praise and blame, is a tool. We do not need a tool to get parents who love their children to be loving parents, or to persuade a man to save from drowning the person he loves most in the world. But we do need a tool to strengthen the tendency toward benevolence which is present in almost all of us, but which also in almost all of us is not strong enough.

In any event, our major concern here is (1): what counts as a moral problem? It is true that the problem of how to achieve a certain end is never, by itself, what we would call a moral problem. On the other hand, it is arguable (and will be argued later in this book) that many if not all moral problems are problems of what end to achieve *and* how one achieves it. One can break down such a problem into two components: the choice of end, and the purely technical component of how one achieves it. But the moral judgement that one makes, 'In this situation I should do such-and-such', contains both components; and one cannot classify it as non-moral just because one of the components is non-moral. Thus there is no reason to conclude that all moral judgements are made on principle regardless of consequences. Nor is there any reason to believe that all decisions on principle regardless of consequences qualify as moral judgements. There are people who would never wear a blue tie with brown shoes on principle, regardless of consequences; but we would not normally consider this a moral judgement, however categorical it may be. Thus Kant's answer to the question of what counts as a moral problem, suggestive though it be, cannot fully be accepted.

A very different answer was given by John Stuart Mill. He held that the peculiar weight and character of moral prescriptivity distinguished morality from what he called 'expediency'. To classify something as morally wrong, in his view, was to imply that punishment was appropriate for someone who did it: the punishment of conscience or of public opinion, if not of the law. Thus moral judgement carries with it a kind of coercion. One can be made to feel guilty, or at least to feel the weight of others' disapproval, if one does the wrong thing. This suggests two theses: that the prescriptivity of moral judgements carries peculiar weight, and that it has a character connected with the impulse towards punishment.

It is only in the light of the first thesis that one can understand the conceptual relocation urged by Mill in *On Liberty*. In this work Mill is at least as concerned with the 'tyranny of the majority' exercised through public opinion as he is with oppression by political functionaries, and this leads him to suggest a way of drawing the line between what should be matters of individual independence and what should be matters of social control: only actions which cause harm to others should be classified as the latter (and thus should be subject to either the physical force of legal penalties or the moral coercion of public opinion). In order to appreciate the revisionary character of Mill's position here, we have to realise that in Mill's time, and to some extent still in ours, many acts not thought to cause harm to others were still subject to the moral coercion of public opinion. Mill wishes to redraw the boundaries of morality in order to lessen pressure on these acts. He certainly does not hold the extreme view that we must express an equally high opinion of all human beings, or that we must like and associate with all equally; on the contrary, he makes it clear that we can reasonably disesteem and avoid those whose non-moral qualities displease us. What he does not say, but clearly assumes, is that this option involves less pressure towards conformity than does moral condemnation, so that the conceptual relocation of acts that do not harm others from the sphere of morality is a liberalising move that reduces pressure. He thinks of moral condemnation as a form of punishment, but does not think of being disliked and avoided by others *per se* as punishment.

It is not clear that Mill was right about this. In America today moral condemnation generally has weight, although perhaps not quite so much as it had in Mill's England. But in a society such as ours, which both is democratic and lacks a strong living tradition of eccentricity, other forms of condemnation or distaste may also have considerable weight. The adolescent who is thought to be odd in dress and manner may suffer more than the adolescent who is thought to commit immoral acts. The problem of *On Liberty* remains: how does one protect individuality from the 'tyranny of the majority'? But conceptually relocating a broad range of conduct, that may offend but does not harm others, outside of the realm of morality may not be a complete solution. It may indeed somewhat diminish social pressure, if sexual activities between consenting adults that do not harm others come to be viewed as not subject to moral judgement; and it would appear that in effect many people nowadays follow Mill in this. But what is not morally condemned can be looked down upon or shunned in other ways; and, as Mill was keenly aware, to remove a kind of conduct from the realm of morality is not to say that one choice is as good as another. My judgement is that we would not classify as a morality a system of condemnation that did not generally involve some considerable weight, but that it is entirely possible that in some societies at certain times other forms of condemnation can have equal or greater weight.

The second thesis, though, may well be correct. Even if being shunned and disesteemed may amount to a kind of punishment, it is questionable whether the inclination to shun and think little of someone is generally a desire to punish. It may be that the judgement that something is morally wrong is normally allied to an impulse to hit out at the offender, and that the judgement that someone is a disagreeable person with low or queer tastes is normally allied to very different impulses. Thus Mill may well be right about the connection between the judgement that some conduct is morally wrong and the sense that punishment of some form is appropriate.

Enough has been said to make it clear that the concept of morality, like almost all of the concepts with which philosophers are concerned, is neither neat nor static. It has become commonplace to say that general terms, other than those developed artificially for use in a special discipline, have meanings that cannot entirely be captured by the traditional mechanism of definition; and this is true of the term 'morality'. We can point to certain things that must be true of anything that counts as a morality, and other things that can never be true of a morality. But we should not expect to find a list of features that moralities, and only moralities, will have. Neither should we assume that the features that we can discern in present morality will all continue to be features of morality indefinitely. The concept of duty does not, by and large, have the same role in the morality of the 1980s as it had in the morality of the 1780s; and certain acts that used to be subject to moral censure are now either not censured or are looked down upon in other ways. Anything at any time that could meet our present standards of what can count as a morality must have certain features: these include some degree of prescriptive weight in its commands, the presence of a core that is concerned with harm to others, perhaps (following Kant somewhat) some degree of emphasis on general principles, and perhaps the link Mill claimed between moral condemnation and a sense that some form of punishment is appropriate. But other features of the morality of some other culture or time can vary. And it might be that some systems of condemnation that we would not quite call morality could have the features just mentioned.

It cannot be emphasised too strongly that to classify something as not a moral matter or not a moral judgement is not to treat it as a matter of indifference or even necessarily as a matter of relative unimportance. We can get a strong sense of this from the ethical philosophy of other cultures. Most of the judgements about the good life contained in Aristotle's *Nicomachean Ethics* or in the *Dialogues* of Plato, or in the classics of Confucian philosophy, are not what we would term moral judgements: that does not mean that they are not important and worth taking seriously. Something like this must be said also about some modern Western works of ethical philosophy. Nietzsche's hostility to morality did not prevent him from having a vision of what kinds of life are worth leading and what kinds are contemptible. The final chapter of G.E. Moore's *Principia Ethica* sets forth a view of the highest humanly attainable values; neither Moore nor any of us would consider these to be moral judgements, or that someone who deliberately eschewed what was most valuable would be classified as having done something morally wrong.

In the light of this confluence of traditions, we should reserve the label 'ethics' for the systematic study or judgement of what is of value and of how we should behave. Morality, then, is a part of ethics, and moral judgements are a subset of ethical judgements. That is, some judgements of how we ought to behave (for example the judgements that we ought not to murder or steal) will be treated as moral judgements; others (for example the judgement that we ought to pursue the contemplative life, or to appreciate beauty wherever we find it) would not be so treated. Perhaps the simplest way of putting the point is to say that morality consists of those parts of ethics that are considered urgent matters of social control.

All ethical judgements about particular cases, whether they are moral or not, have conclusive prescriptivity. That is, it is always true that what is ethically right is what one should permit oneself to do; what is ethically wrong is what one should not do; what is ethically best is what one should pursue; and what is ethically bad is what one should avoid. On the other hand, occassionally one should act in a way which genuinely in that case is rude if, say, this prevents great suffering, or helps to right important wrongs. Judgements of etiquette have prescriptivity but not conclusive prescriptivity; they tell how one should behave, assuming that there are no pressing reasons of another sort for behaving differently. Similarly aesthetic and practical judgements tell one what to do, but only if there are no pressing reasons of another sort for behaving otherwise. But pressing reasons of all sorts must be able to be considered in an ethical judgement of how one should behave, and thus there is no room for such a judgement to be outweighed by outside factors. If it appears that moral considerations can be outweighed in some cases by, say, 'purely practical' considerations, all this means is that in such cases factors that normally would be decisive (for example that one promised to do such-and-such) are outweighed by other factors, so that an action of a kind that normally would be morally wrong is not morally wrong in this case. In the next chapter we shall discuss the widely shared moral judgement that there are special circumstances in which one is justified in breaking general rules such as the one governing keeping promises.

If both moral and other ethical judgements have conclusive prescriptivity, then why are not all important ethical judgements included within morality? Why could we not, for example, consider it morally obligatory to pursue the contemplative life if one has a chance? Part of the answer is that we could. But a society in which decisions about the style of one's life were subject to what Mill called 'moral coercion' would seem significantly less free than ours. It is true, as was remarked earlier, that non-moral deviations are sometimes subject to great social pressure; but often they are not, and people who eschew the contemplative life seem in our society to suffer very little pressure. It might be argued by some that a society in which no decisions were subject to moral coercion would be freest of all; but such a society would be filled with danger, and arguably not a society at all. The dangers to most of us of allowing people an uncoerced choice of whether to pursue the contemplative life are much less serious than of allowing an uncoerced choice of whether or not to kill people one dislikes.

This is only part of the answer. If morality is a form of social control, then it must have certain features in order to function effectively. Three general requirements must be met: (1) morality must be able to be taught to, remembered by, and applied by the great majority of the population; (2) morality must not ask too much, and correct moral choices must be within the power of the great majority of the population; and (3) moral transgressions must be readily identifiable and describable.

(1) In order to be shared by almost everyone in a society, morality must have a centre that is not too complicated or subtle. From this point of view, highly general moral rules without explicit qualifications, such as those of the Ten Commandments, are ideal. The reader should note that there is no requirement here that *all* of morality consist of such general rules. A morality can be shared to a high degree by almost everyone, in a simple understanding, while some also maintain a more sophisticated and qualified interpretation of it. Almost all of the world's great religions are shared by their adherents

in much this way. Thus it is possible for a society to have a morality which centres on simple general rules, which are taught to children and remembered and applied by adults, without its being generally agreed that every moral problem can be solved by straightforward and simple application of these rules. We shall discuss this further in the next chapter.

(2) Morality cannot set too high a standard and function effectively as morality. It may well be that, as Jesus said, a man who wishes to be perfect will give all he has to the poor. But that cannot be expected of the great majority of people, and thus in societies like ours it functions not as part of morality but as something 'supererogatory': as a saintly or heroic act which goes beyond what morality asks.

Some demands are difficult to meet because they require a close and continuous attention to the details of one's life, and thus do not leave room for what most people would consider the minimum degree of personal relaxation. Demands, in various religious traditions, to purify one's thoughts have this character. A life of monitoring one's thoughts, to see that they are properly focused and that impurities are purged, can have a high value; but it cannot be expected of most people, and hence cannot be made a requirement of morality. Our morality tends to focus on single acts, viewed as discrete and fairly disconnected from the rest of life: for example on someone's choice of whether or not to murder, or to steal. This is very manageable for the great majority of people, because it leaves most of life – everything apart from the occasional moments of moral decision – free for the pursuit of whatever personal goals one has. One can imagine a morality that condemned certain habits and mental sets more freely than ours does, and that demanded that people frequently examine the general quality of their lives; but any morality that went far in this direction would also be in danger of demanding too much, and hence of not functioning effectively as a morality.

(3) Anyone who holds the simple view that morality is concerned with the general prevention of harm to others should reflect on the fact that often the greatest harm is produced by subtly flawed personal relations, between parents and children, or between spouses, lovers, or friends, that are not commonly brought within the purview of morality. A parent, for example, can seriously damage the self-esteem and the future life of a child by subtle details of inattention, or of too much attention given in the wrong way, or by slighting or indifferent remarks. The harm done by a petty thief pales in comparison; and yet stealing is morally wrong, whereas we do not commonly say that it is morally wrong to be a poor parent of one of the kinds just described.

In some cases, of course, it is possible to say that the person who harms others through subtly flawed personal relations does not know what he or she is doing, and this is a ground for distinction between such a person and a thief (who commonly does know what he or she is doing). We normally do not pass judgement on what people are not aware of committing. However, there certainly are many cases in which people who harm others through subtly flawed personal relations do know what they are doing. There is no dramatic and simple label like 'stealing' for this kind of harming others; and, for this reason and also because what is involved frequently is a pattern of behaviour rather than discrete acts, and because it is the result of thousands of little decisions rather than a few big ones, it is possible to put out of one's mind just what it is that one is doing.

The exclusion of harm to others of this kind from the realm of morality is over-determined. First of all, morality as a social mechanism requires the normal possibility of a common vision of what is being condemned. We can normally agree when stealing or murder has taken place. But harm such that some degree of sensitivity and perceptiveness is required to recognise the damage, and how the damage was caused, cannot be treated in this way. Secondly, for reasons already given, it does not seem too much to require that discrete acts of certain specified sorts not be performed; a demand that patterns of behaviour be modified asks a great deal more. Finally we have, increasingly since Mill's time, a sense that there is an area of private life which should not be subject to moral coercion except for very clear and pressing reasons. In cases of harm of the sort under discussion, the reasons are rarely clear to everyone's satisfaction; and if the victims are consenting adults or members of a family, there is a special reluctance to license moral invasion. It should be remembered that physical harm is both more dramatic and more easily displayed to everyone's satisfaction than psychological harm. Even psychological harm can be subject to moral condemnation if it is dramatic and clear-cut enough to be labelled as, say, child abuse. Otherwise, important though it may be, it lies outside of the purview of morality.

One reason for dwelling on all of this is that recent ethical philosophers have so thoroughly confined their attention to a narrow range of examples, drawn with reference to the centre of morality, that it has been possible to think that all important decisions of better or worse, or all decisions involving the prevention of harm, are moral decisions. We must see morality for what it is. Its importance, and the human need for it, can be recognised adequately even if we also recognise the importance of what lies outside morality.

In any event, none of the discussion of this chapter should be taken as suggesting any of the positions that have gone under names like 'subjectivism', 'emotivism', 'relativism', or more generally 'non-cognitivism'. It is important to remind ourselves continuously that morality is a human invention, that it is designed to do some jobs but not others, and of course that moral concepts are human creations, and that the very concept of morality itself has cultural roots. But one can say equally that the sciences are human inventions, designed to do some jobs but not others, and that scientific concepts are human creations, and that the very concept of 'the sciences' itself has cultural roots. All of this is compatible with saying that cognitive standards apply in the sciences, and that there is important scientific knowledge. This is not the place to speculate on how the sciences of intelligent beings on other planets could differ from ours. It is enough to say that there are intermediate positions between, at one extreme, the view that there is a single objectively best way of structuring knowledge and, at the other extreme, the relativistic view that all consistent systems of knowledge are equally valid. It scarcely need be said, also, that correct claims can be made within a conceptual framework, such as those of the sciences or of ethics. Nothing in this chapter implies that it is not the case that, for example, torture really is morally wrong.

NOTES AND REFERENCES

The two most prominent philosophers to have written about the demands of morality are Immanuel Kant and John Stuart Mill. Kant directly approaches this subject in *Foundations of the Metaphysics of Morals*. This is a powerful and highly controversial work. In it Kant makes clear what the special characteristics of the moral are, and also provides an *a priori* mechanism (the categorical imperative) for morally testing principles of action. Kant is especially clear that a perfectly good or 'holy' will is not 'constrained' by moral laws (pages 30–1 of the Bobbs-Merrill edition of Lewis White Beck's translation). Moral laws are validated by the categorical imperative, which Kant (p. 33) calls 'the imperative of morality'.

The two works of John Stuart Mill discussed in the chapter are *Utilitarianism* and *On Liberty*. *Utilitarianism* provides an outline and general discussion of utilitarianism, an ethical theory which combines the view that the consequences of actions are what matter with the claim that consequences are to be weighed in terms of their contribution to pleasure or happiness or to the elimination of pain and unhappiness. As a skilful writer, Mill anticipates likely criticisms; one likely criticism is that the utilitarian concern for consequences sets a standard that could be met by an unjust act that increased the net total of human happiness; and so the final chapter is devoted to showing that utilitarianism does not conflict with a reasonable approach to justice. This requires Mill to say what justice is, and on the way to this he must distinguish more generally morality from what he calls 'expediency'. The realm of expediency can be understood to include all choices which can be better or worse, but in which the worse choice would not be termed morally wrong. According to Mill, the distinction between morality and expediency is such that we classify under morality cases in which the worse choice ought to be punished (either by law or conscience or public opinion); cases in which we do not think the worse choice ought to be punished can be assigned to expediency. *On Liberty* is a defence of individualism against excessive pressures on the part of society. Some of these pressures are institutional and obvious: for example, legal pressure directed against freedom of speech and of thought. But Mill also is concerned about extra-legal pressure, about the 'moral coercion of public opinion' (page 13 of the Bobbs-Merrill edition edited by Currin Shields). He argues that individuals should not be subject to this moral coercion as long as their actions do not harm others. However he also says (p. 94) that 'there is a degree of folly, and a degree of what may be called . . . lowness or depravation of taste, which though it cannot justify doing harm to the person who manifests it, renders him necessarily and properly a subject of distaste, or in extreme cases, even of contempt'. This distaste or contempt is presumably not as weighty as the 'moral coercion of public opinion'.

Good sources for Nietzsche's view of morality are *Beyond Good and Evil* and *Thus Spoke Zarathustra*. I interpret Nietzsche as opposed to morality because of his dislike of use of characteristic moral terms, such as 'good' and 'evil', and because of his resentment of societal pressure (of the sort that morality represents) on remarkable individuals. In fact Nietzsche himself does not provide anything like a morality: there are, for example, no rules or principles transgression of which he thinks should make one feel guilty. But he does provide an elaborate guide towards what he thinks would be a life of the highest quality, a life indeed worth repeating endlessly; and in this sense he is an ethical philosopher, even if he is not a moral philosopher.

Thomas Hobbes's view of the origin of law and morality is presented in Chapters 13–15 of *Leviathan*. Lenin speaks of the withering away of the state in 'State and revolution', reprinted in Robert V. Daniels, *A Documentary History of Communism*, Vol. 1 (New York, 1962). The withering away will occur as people 'gradually become accustomed to observing the elementary rules of intercourse'. However, Lenin does not 'deny the possibility and inevitability of excesses on the part of individual persons, or the need to suppress such excesses'. But 'no special apparatus of suppression is needed for this' (p. 102). Morality, fortified by spontaneous coercion on the part of the moral community, will be enough.

The example of the man clasping his hands three times an hour is taken from Philippa Foot's 'Moral beliefs' (*Proceedings of the Aristotelian Society*, 1958), which is reprinted in a collection of her essays, *Virtues and Vices* (Berkeley, 1978). Other important essays in that collection that are particularly relevant to this chapter include 'Morality as a system of hypothetical imperatives' and 'Are moral considerations overriding?' Hare's thesis of the prescriptivity of ethical judgements is contained in *Freedom and Reason* (Oxford, 1963). A classic discussion of the 'supererogatory' is contained in J.O. Urmson's 'Saints and heroes', in A. I. Melden (ed.), *Essays in Moral Philosophy* (Seattle, 1958). Discussions of the objectivity of ethics and other forms of human knowledge are contained in my *Ethical Knowledge* (London, 1970), 'Precision in history' (*Mind*, 1975), and 'Is the nature of physical reality unknowable?' (*American Philosophical Quarterly*, 1978). Finally I should direct the reader to P.F. Strawson's brilliant essay, the influence of which on much of this chapter will be manifest, 'Social morality and individual ideals' (*Philosophy*, 1961).

Chapter 2

Morality as Law

It may seem that, up to this point, we have skirted the most distinctive feature of morality: its generality. If we look at the actual workings of morality, we are again and again presented with cases of people solving moral problems by means of general rules and principles. Furthermore, it is frequently the recognition that the problem at hand is a moral one that leads immediately to an appeal to a general framework. Rules and principles are experienced by conscientious people as binding: one's conscience tells one, in the terms of a general framework, what one *must* do. On the basis of all this, which even causal observation discloses as characteristic of the phenomenon of morality, it is very tempting to think of morality as consisting of laws, rather like the laws to be found in legal codes. A view much like this was held by Immanuel Kant; and, rooted as it is in common sense, and descriptive of common sense, it cannot be entirely wrong. In this chapter we shall explore the respects in which morality can be viewed as law.

Let us begin with Kant. The centrepiece of Kant's moral philosophy is the categorical imperative, which in the *Foundations of the Metaphysics of Morals* is presented in three formulations, intended as three different ways of stating the same moral requirement. The first, and most famous, formulation is that one should act only according to that maxim which one can at the same time will to become a universal law. In the second formulation the categorical imperative tells one that human beings, including oneself, should always be treated as ends rather than as means. This is often interpreted as a principle of respect for persons. In the third formulation the categorical imperative tells us to act as if we lived in an ideal moral community: in other words, even if in fact other people are not entirely moral you should keep your own standards up as if they were.

The categorical imperative is not itself a moral rule: it is a device for testing moral rules. Kant simply assumed, without argument, that the rules to be tested were broad. For moral purposes one case of stealing or lying is much the same as another. From Kant's remarks on this, and from the examples he presents in *Foundations of the Metaphysics of Morals*, it would appear that the moral rules that can be validated by the categorical imperative are exception-free as well as broad: for example, 'Never commit suicide', 'Never make false promises'. The view that morality centres on rules that admit of no exceptions has been known as 'rigorism'. Kant at times sounds very much like a rigorist; although commentators have disagreed about whether he really was one, and there are hints of a non-rigorist position in the *Metaphysical Principles of Virtue*.

In any event, rigorism has had a bad name for some time. It has come to be common sense that the broad familiar moral rules governing such matters as lying, promise-breaking, and stealing have at least imaginable exceptions. That is, even if a case in which the rule should be broken is so rare that one of us is unlikely to encounter it in real life, an ingenious philosopher can create an imaginary case of which most of us would say, 'Yes, in those circumstances it would be right to steal (lie, or break a promise).' Thus Kant's rigorism, if he was a rigorist, has been very little respected. More respect has been paid to the formal requirements of morality implicit in the categorical imperative.

We shall postpone discussion of the categorical imperative, and of similar fundamental and formal moral principles, until the next chapter; and in this chapter we shall concentrate on moral rules. It is very hard to shake the sense that rules are central to morality, and rigorism is the neatest expression of that sense. It has been ingeniously revived lately by Alan Donagan, as part of a defence of what he calls the 'common morality'. Donagan argues that the network of rules included in the common morality is, properly understood, adequate to all moral problems, and that, properly understood, the rules are exception-free.

Rigorism can seem most plausible with regard to moral rules whose normal formulation centres on terms that are themselves morally loaded. It is open to argument whether murder is ever, even in extreme imaginable cases, permissible: we normally would not term an act of killing 'murder' if we thought it justified. Something similar is at least arguable about theft, and thus there is room for a case that murder and theft are never justified, based on our tendency to deny that a case we think exceptional actually is one of 'murder' or 'theft' (although the case is much stronger for murder than for theft). In any case this does not help someone who is deliberating whether to kill someone or take someone's property (say during wartime), and wonders whether the action contemplated would count as murder or theft.

What of moral rules that use somewhat more neutral terms? Promising is a good test case here. Donagan's view is that it is impermissible for anybody to break a freely made promise to do something in itself morally permissible. Of course there may be pressing reasons to break a promise, but it is understood implicitly that the moral rule does not require one to keep a promise in cases in which these pressing reasons are to be found. Thus the moral rule, with the tacit conditions that qualify it understood correctly, gives the correct answer in every case to which it applies, and at the same time accords with common sense. The apparent exceptions turn out to be allowed by the rule itself, once we understand its true meaning.

The inspiration for this manoeuvre may be found in the example in which Wittgenstein imagines someone telling him to teach the children a game. He teaches them to shoot dice, and provokes the protest that that was not what was meant. In much the same way, if in a room with many windows I ask you to let in some fresh air, and you shoot a hole in the wall with a howitzer, I can plausibly protest that that is not what I meant. A woman who says 'You should not be late for appointments' also can protest, if you rush past a drowning man in order to be on time for an appointment, that that is not what she meant. It is with this kind of implicit meaning that Donagan argues that what might appear to be exceptions are actually allowed for by familiar moral rules.

There are at least two ways to interpret our sense of moral requirements. One (Donagan's) is to say that what people mean when they affirm a familiar moral rule, such as the one that governs promise-keeping, tacitly subsumes the (apparent) exceptions. Another is to say that there is by now so much consensus to the effect that the rules have exceptions that we normally cannot seriously believe that someone intends us to follow the rule in the most drastic exceptional cases: that is not because of the meaning of the rule, but rather because of a substantive consensus about how far it should be followed. Plainly a great deal depends on who is doing the talking. Just as there are some who would include dice-shooting among the games to be taught to the children, so also there are rigid martinets who would require that one keep a promise in any conceivable case. But people of these sorts are rare. Normally we assume some degree of agreement, at least about extreme cases, that the rules can be broken. Evidence for the second interpretation is found in the fact that such extreme cases are generally described as cases of breaking the rule, even when this is agreed to be justified.

In any event, the consensus about the application of familiar moral rules to exceptional cases – whether it is one about meaning or a substantive one – is not very detailed. Virtually everyone agrees that you should not rush past a drowning man in order to keep a promise, but there is much less agreement as to the degree of threatened financial loss that would excuse breaking a promise. Even if it is true that moral rules contain a tacit rider to the effect of 'except in extreme cases', there is no consensus, either about meaning or in moral judgement, as to the boundaries of what count as extreme cases, or as to how cases that might appear serious but not extreme should be judged. Thus, in the absence of such a detailed consensus, even if it is granted that moral rules are to be understood as containing tacit riders, we are in no position to say that moral rules acceptably solve all problems, for the simple reason that (for many problems) we are then in no position to say what answers follow from the moral rules. A rigorism in which rules like 'Do not break promises' are taken at face value is preposterous, but it also is definite: we know roughly what we are signing up for if we accept it. A rigorism in which moral rules include infinitely complex conditions which will remain forever tacit losses in definiteness and clarity what it gains in plausibility.

There are only two ways in which a rigorism can be maintained in which what might have been exceptions are subsumed under rules. Either the whole moral code must be spelled out, so that we know and can articulate the sub-rules that tell us when a rule does or does not apply, as well as knowing and articulating rules of priority that tell us how to judge apparent conflicts between moral rules, etc.; or a clear and definite mechanism for dealing with apparent exceptions and other complications must be articulated. The first alternative would give us a complete and adequate morality in the form of a code; the second would give us a science of interpreting, adjusting, and qualifying moral rules.

Both of these ways of saving rigorism have had their devotees in recent years. No advocate of the complete and entirely adequate rigorist moral code has, however, produced the code. Because of this disappointing failure, one must remain sceptical about the prospects for any such attempt. The second way, which is casuistry, has also had disappointing failures. Casuistry in its historical form might be described (unsympathetically) as the art of verbal ingenuity to fiddle with difficult moral cases to make them come out right. The *Schaff-Herzog Encyclopedia of Religious Knowledge*, a Protestant compilation published in the nineteenth century, in its article on casuistry comments on its historical development: 'The cases became more and more intricate, the solutions more and more subtle; the power of conscience to give a clear and ready verdict was blunted and confounded . . .' The defence of a complicated rigorism requires more success than this.

A more straightforward view of the limitations on the use of the moral rules to solve problems is this. A wide range of moral problems can be solved simply and easily by means of rules. In ordinary cases, to be told that doing such-and-such would involve breaking a promise is enough for one to know that one should not do such-and-such. But from time to time there are cases in which unusual factors make it seem plausible that one should break a promise, or violate some other familiar and generally valid moral rule. We approach these cases, typically, not by scrutinising hidden meanings in the rule itself but rather by looking at factors of the case at hand. We weigh the importance of the factors that might justify us in breaking the rule. This requires a good deal of judgement, which in turn must be founded in experience.

Just how one should approach such perplexing cases will be discussed further in Chapters 5 and 8. It should be remarked now, however, that the account just summarised is essentially that found both in Aristotle's ethics and in the classics of Confucian philosophy. In both it is adumbrated in terms of the importance of following the mean. Casual readers of Aristotle, or of the Confucian *Doctrine of the Mean*, frequently misunderstand this as a bland admonition to be moderate. But what the doctrine says is this. There are some virtues which consist of always (when the occasion arises) behaving in a certain way, or of never doing a certain kind of thing. For example, any Confucian will always be kind and loyal to her or his parents; about adultery, Aristotle remarks tartly that it is not a question of performing it at the right time, with the right woman, etc. However, many virtues are matters of doing something only at the right time, and in the right way. The mean that these embody is a policy intermediate between always doing a certain kind of thing and never doing it. The courageous person, for example, does not (like the foolhardy person) always advance into danger even when the risks outweigh the likely gains; nor does the courageous person always (like the coward) retreat. To follow the mean effectively requires a flexible conduct based on judgement of the particular case and of what is appropriate to it.

The fact remains that moral rules not only are devices for solving moral problems, but also provide us with reasons to justify our choices. If we are asked 'Why is X wrong?' normally 'X would involve breaking a promise' or 'X would inflict needless pain' serves as a conclusive reason. In short, morality contains within itself a logic as well as decision procedures, and moral rules have a unique and powerful role within this logic. It may not be immediately clear how we can square this unique and powerful role with what we have been saying about exceptions to moral rules.

One way of seeing the problem is to consider this. If 'X would involve breaking a promise' is a reason for 'X is wrong', is that not because 'X is wrong' in some sense *follows* from 'X would involve breaking a promise'? But if that is the case, then the requirements of logic tell us that what is true in one instance must be true universally: 'X is wrong' must always follow from 'X would involve breaking a promise'. Thus we seem to be back with rigorism.

There are two ways in which we might be able to do justice to the use of moral rules as reasons while escaping rigorism. One way is to regard reasons like 'X would involve breaking a promise' as elliptical. The reason, in this view, does not constitute a purely logical move: it combines argument with a pointing manoeuvre. The full meaning is something like 'X would involve breaking a promise, and there is not extraordinarily much to be said in favour of X' or 'X would involve breaking a promise, and is not a special case'. The reason can be taken as conclusive only because one looks at X and sees that it is not a special case.

Alternatively, the logic of appeals to moral rules can be taken as probabilistic. An analogy can be made with aesthetic reasoning. Aesthetic rules also have exceptions, but a critic can point to features of a work of art such that works that have such features are usually bad, and thus build a case to justify an unfavourable evaluation. Ever since the revolutions of early twentieth-century art it has become common-place to regard the operative word in aesthetic canons as 'usually' rather than 'always' or 'never'. Thus one can point to features of a work that count as flaws, that are such that usually works with those features are bad, while not foreclosing the possibility that a work could be constructed with those features that was somehow good. The critic's reasons can make it seem highly probable that a work is bad (or good), but ultimately one looks at the work itself. It may be that reasons in moral argument that are derived from moral rules operate in much this way.

Whichever of these accounts is correct, it is clear that the kinds of reasons we are discussing do not in any sense *prove* that something is right or wrong. Even someone who accepts the rule from which the reason is derived, and who regards the reason as strong, need not regard it as in every possible case conclusive. I can agree that (gener-ally) promises ought to be kept, and accept 'X would involve breaking a promise' as a strong reason against X, without accepting it as in every case conclusive. Thus it would be wrong to regard the use of moral rules in reasons as playing a part in a logic such that anyone who accepts a reason must in every possible case accept the conclusion that the reason supports. We need not return to rigorism.

Rigorism emerges, in the arguments I have been presenting, as a too neat answer both to problems about the nature of moral rules and to problems about the nature of moral reasoning. We must be careful not to be too neat in our rejection of rigorism. It is important to remind ourselves that rigorism has roots in the nature of morality, that general rules do appear to have a central function in morality, and that people of good will often experience these as binding with the force of law.

One way in which we can begin to do justice to all of this is, as it were, to re-invent morality, so that, building morality from the ground up, we can see the role that general rules need to play. We should, however, guard against misunderstandings. When we talk about the functioning of a moral system, and of what is required for an effective morality, it may sound as if any morality is something that is accepted throughout a society. We all know that it is possible for an individual or for a small group to hold moral views, and to be governed by a morality, not widely shared in their society. The point to bear in mind, however, is that (however diffident people are about persuading others that their moral viewpoint is correct) to hold that something is morally wrong is to hold that others, if they were more intelligent, sensible, or decent, would recognise that it is morally wrong. Thus any morality, even if it is held by only one person or a small group, is potentially a contender for the role of dominant societal morality. Some of the standards by which a morality is judged – the ones we will discuss in this chapter and the next – are functional: they concern how well a morality works, or can work, in a societal role. This is not, however, to deny that other standards are appropriate as well, so that ultimately we can ask not only whether a morality is functional but also whether, say, its functioning contributes to the well-being of sentient beings. This is akin to asking about a scientific theory, not only whether it is coherent and offers genuine explanations and predictions of events (whether it does function as a scientific theory), but also whether it explains and predicts well.

Thus, by examining what a morality must be in order to function effectively (as a dominant societal morality) we put to the side possible judgements, based on considerations we will explore in Part Three, that some functional moralities are superior to others. We still can learn a great deal about the nature of morality merely by asking what is required for a morality to function effectively.

Let us start from the social function that a dominant morality must play. An effective morality must be understood, mastered, and usually followed by the great majority of a population. It must manage this in order to contribute to the kind of elementary security of which Hobbes spoke. To be understood and mastered by the great majority, a morality cannot be (at least in its core) too complicated. The things it picks out to be condemned must be readily identifiable by most people: overt actions rather than thoughts, pronounced and discrete changes in people's lives rather than the subtle workings of a style of personal relationships. Because an important part of the functioning of a moral system is its use in generating social pressure on forbidden activities, it is important that a morality focus on items that permit of a sharable vision of what is to be condemned. Subtle workings of a style of personal relationships, again, are inappropriate because they are too easily subject to varying interpretations. Compliance with an effective morality need not be entirely universal, nor need the appeal of the morality be deeply felt by everyone. We cannot count on everyone, say, never to steal; and it may be that, given a ring of invisibility, most people would finally bring themselves to steal. But property institutions along with the rule against theft would be impossible unless the great majority of people were most of the time not prepared to steal. An effective morality requires at least a slight general appeal and widespread compliance.

The need for a simple core of morality becomes especially apparent when we realise that we cannot wait to instil morality until people are adults with mature intellects. Even children can be dangerous, and furthermore the moral behaviour of adults is determined not only by intellectual considerations but also by the habits of youth. Aristotle especially stressed this point. Consequently we need a very simple core of morality which is suitable for transmission to young children, and which can be remembered by them when they are grown.

Moral rules fill this need admirably. Rules saying that one should not murder, steal, break promises, or inflict needless suffering are suitable even for the comprehension of very young children. They are easy to remember. It is an interesting question whether the part of ethics that concerns the most suitable goals of life, the part that comprehends Aristotle's recommendation of the contemplative life and G.E. Moore's highly favourable evaluation of affectionate relationships with people who are worthy of them, would lend itself to formulation in general rules as readily as morality has. But there is no need for that part of ethics to be so formulated. We are not threatened if people take the wrong view of the contemplative life or of the value of affection as we are if they take the wrong view of murder or theft. And it may be, also, that what is wrong in murder is easier for a child to comprehend than what is desirable in a contemplative life.

Some people may respond by conceding this point, but also by saying that moral rules are indeed for children and just for children. This view has gained strength among people who have been impressed by the exceptions to moral rules, and also by the dangers of always applying moral rules rigidly and mechanically. Such people sometimes say that adults can put moral rules entirely to the side, and can be governed by a morality that views each situation in its own terms and judges each possible course of action on its own merits.

This is naive, however, for a number of reasons. One is that moral rightness or wrongness is not usually luminous: it does not usually jump out to our vision as we inspect a scene. The comprehension that the average person who is not governed by moral rules has of a moral problem is rather like the average person's comprehension of a Jackson Pollock painting. So, first of all, moral rules function as orientation devices. They enable us to pick out salient features of what is being morally judged. Without such orientation devices, most of us would be at a loss, and even the cleverest and most virtuous would find it difficult to make the quick decisions that are sometimes required.

We may put to the side, for a moment, the question of whether any of us is all that clever and virtuous. Another matter has to be taken up first. We must remind ourselves that morality is a social device, and not just an aid for individuals such as ourselves in solving problems. We must remind ourselves also of the full implications of calling morality a social device. Many people who are attracted to individualism think of society as a 'them', as a grey force pressing on them in their personal lives. Because we can have many moods, and feel the appeal of conflicting ideals at almost the same time, many of the same people also deplore the dwindling, in recent times, of a sense of community, and of a shared outlook on the problems of life. They should realise that morality as a social device is not just a source of pressure; it also is an important element of cohesion, in strengthening a sense of community and of a shared outlook. This is an important part of how an effective morality has to function.

Thus, even if it were the case that an individual here or there could function markedly very well without moral rules, a community cannot; and the individual who dispenses with moral rules is to that extent cut off from the community. The most obvious function of moral rules within a community is to delineate what is permitted and what is forbidden. But this requires, as we have been pointing out, other functions, which include making possible a shared vision of the actions and events that are subject to moral judgement. Moral concepts structure the reality perceived by the people who use them. In a complicated series of events in which one element is that someone takes your watch or your camera without your permission, someone who has mastered and remembered the moral rule about theft will experience that element as salient in a way in which someone who has not mastered or has forgotten the rule perhaps will not. Morality can function effectively only because, in a situation in which your watch or camera is stolen, you can normally count on most of the people around you seeing the situation in just those terms.

Someone might, of course, remember the moral rules of childhood, and use them in communicating with others, but personally solve moral problems without their aid. It is time, though, to question this. The argument presented earlier in this chapter concerning rigorism was that *some* moral problems cannot be solved purely by application of moral rules. Even then, though, it was not suggested that moral rules would be entirely useless in one's approach to these difficult and unusual problems. Just how one should approach such problems will be discussed more fully in Chapters 5 and 8. What I wish to argue now is that it is impractical and dangerous for an individual human being (at least one who has not become a saint) to approach *all* moral problems without the aid of moral rules.

How indeed might one totally dispense with moral rules? One suggestion is that if one simply acts always in a loving way moral rules become unnecessary; indeed morality itself becomes unnecessary. There are two problems with this. One is that those of us who have not become saints, who retain the imperfections of human nature, may have impulses of hostility or irritation as well as loving thoughts; a personal ethics of love may have the effect of teaching its adherent to disguise hostility and irritation as forms of love. One of the strengths of conventional morality is the openness to criticism that it creates: if we steal or break promises, this can be readily seen by others and by ourselves, and criticisms can be readily formulated. If I persuade myself that I determine my actions not by moral rules but out of love, what I do that is spiteful, wounding, or merely self-aggrandising and unctuous can be recognised by some but probably not by everyone, and almost certainly not by myself, and the possibilities both of external criticism and of self-criticism are blunted.

The second problem is this. Some moral decisions involve the possibility of doing good or harm to some person or persons, with no significant countervailing harm or good to others; such are decisions of whether to save someone's life, or of whether to steal from or murder one's neighbour. A personal ethics of love will easily tell one to save the life, and not to steal from or murder one's neighbour; but then moral rules also work easily and well in such cases. In more difficult cases, there is a choice of goods or a choice of evils: by breaking my word to A I can help B to avert danger, or by stealing medicine from a druggist I can cure my sick wife. If, whatever we do, some people will suffer, how is an ethics of love to operate? In more difficult cases, we need priorities; we need to be told how to weigh the factors involved. We also, it should be said, need to be reminded of the importance of less obvious factors: the long-term social effects of breaking promises or of bending the law can be important, even if they make little immediate appeal to our emotional responses. Now the business of weighing factors relevant to moral judgement, and of giving appropriate consideration to long-term, more subtle effects of our actions, is difficult; and nothing to be said in this book will amount to a recipe for solution of every case. But we can see that moral rules make at least a start of picking out relevant factors, and of signalling that they are to be given serious weight. A personal ethics of love allows for the possibility of an undifferentiated experience of the whole complex of factors relevant to a moral problem. One then has an emotional response to the whole, and makes the moral decision accordingly. An analogue would be a personal epistemology of intuition: one solves any problem, whether one of astrophysics or of sociology, by spreading all of the data before one, and then waiting for an answer to pop into one's head.

One advantage of a morality that centres on general rules over one that dispenses with general rules is, simply, the likelihood of a higher percentage of acceptable answers. A morality that dispenses with general rules, such as a personal ethics of love, runs the twin dangers of self-deception and of intellectual sloppiness. Perhaps a saint can consistently will more good than harm. But most of us run the risk of thinking that we are loving when we are something else. And, even if we are pure of heart, is there any reason to suppose that our purity will be more efficacious in dealing with complicated questions of morality than it would be in dealing with complex questions of physics? A genuinely pure person must still isolate relevant factors, weigh them, and determine the importance of the benefits and hurts to be inflicted, in arriving at a moral decision in a complex case. The familiar apparatus of general rules provides at least a starting-point in this process. As we have pointed out, in a very wide range of less complicated cases it provides more than just a starting-point.

One final advantage of centring morality on general rules should be noted. It would be a mistake to overemphasise the role of cognitive factors in moral life and to neglect the role of habits and inclinations. It is entirely possible for someone to recognise that a certain action is wrong, and yet cheerfully perform it without any hesitation. It is to avoid this possibility that we try to give children the habits of behaving in a virtuous manner, and hope that they will ultimately take intrinsic pleasure in behaving virtuously and will find the prospect of behaving immorally to be intrinsically painful. Traditional moral rules serve as a handy device for structuring habits and attitudes. Actions are grouped together as cases of promise-breaking, or of inflicting needless suffering on others; and we get in the habit of not doing those kinds of things, and fall into an attitude of finding the prospect of our doing them painful.

Even if a moral rule has possible exceptions, it can be very useful for us to be in the habit of following the moral rule, and to feel distaste at the thought of breaking it. It is not only that the habit, and our distaste, can protect us against crude temptations to do what we know is wrong. There are more subtle temptations to be guarded against. There are cases in which we very much wish to think that a case at hand is an exception to a moral rule, which we know can have some exceptions, and our judgement of the case is clouded by our inclinations. Once people realise that moral rules have exceptions, there is a great risk that far too many will be claimed. The only solution to this (short of falling back into rigorism) is to instil moral rules in such a way that people feel inhibited about breaking them, and that when people do break them there is a psychic cost to be borne. If I am in the habit of keeping my promises, and feel uneasy at the prospect of breaking one, I still may encounter cases in which reflectively I judge that I ought to break a promise. But there will be fewer such cases than if I were not inhibited about breaking promises. And one of the marks of the power of the moral rule over me is that afterwards I will feel badly about having broken a promise, even if I continue to judge that this was justified.

Let me summarise the points just made about the relation of moral rules to the function of morality. Morality is a social device to minimise certain sorts of behaviour, especially behaviour that threatens the security of members of the community. In order to fulfil this function, it must have at least a core which can be taught to children, which can form the basis of habits of compliance, and which makes possible quick shared recognition of things to be condemned. Broad general rules are ideally suited to serve as this core. Without such general rules we could not so well remember what is morally expected of us, share perceptions of the morally salient features of situations with others, or form habits of not doing certain kinds of things (or at least of not doing them lightly). General rules have a continuing usefulness in moral problem-solving, and it is questionable whether any of us could do without them entirely. But it is as starting-points, both in moral development and in a shared consciousness, that their necessity is clearest.

If we are well brought up, we continue through life to feel the pull of moral rules on us; they seem to operate as internal commands, which to some extent we continue to endorse. It is very tempting, because of this, to think of ourselves as somehow legislating the moral rules, and because of the respect we give them and the uneasiness we feel at the prospect of violating them to think of the moral rules as like laws. This brings us to the title of this chapter. Morality *is* law, in some sense. But in philosophy few things are as simple as they first seem. It is time to address ourselves to the points of connection, the similarities, and the differences between morality and law.

Clearly both the origins and the functions of morality and law have much in common. Both are social devices designed, among other things, to promote security. In modern times law has carried with it a formal apparatus of interpretation and enforcement, and there is a widespread sense that some things which 'ought not to be allowed' yet do not warrant the application of this sometimes cumbersome and heavily intrusive apparatus. Thus it is widely thought that there are actions which are immoral but not illegal. Even in the mildest and most liberal system of law there are likely to be actions which are illegal but not immoral. Some (for example illegal parking) must be regulated but simply are not heinous enough to be termed immoral. Sometimes also there is a social point in holding someone 'legally responsible' (which in many cases means, in effect, financially responsible) for actions which rest on mistakes or bad luck and which we would not blame morally. Thus law and morality diverge, and it would be very hard to argue that they should not diverge. But, at the core, the actions that the law comes down hardest upon are the actions that we also consider immoral, and it is hard to resist the view that in their core areas law and morality point towards the same goals. One gets a strong sense of this by looking at any early code such as the Ten Commandments, of which it is not entirely easy to distinguish the legal and the moral functions.

Law also shares with morality two important features. One, which we shall discuss in the next chapter, is interpersonal neutrality. Modern legal codes apply 'irrespective of persons', and clearly any moral code worthy of the name will do so as well. The other feature is that it is a desideratum in a law, and also in a moral rule, that it be formulated as broadly and simply as possible; while ignorance of the law is no excuse, we hope to facilitate knowledge of the law. But laws, again like moral rules, in their simplest form may seem to function better for certain kinds of cases than for others; and hence there is a natural tendency both in law and in morality to refine by means of introducing complications. Casuistry of course is the extreme expression of this tendency in morality, and casuistry would appear in part to be a phenomenon of moralists imitating lawyers.

Complications are introduced, both in law and in systems of moral rules, because there are cases which do not seem to be decided well if the laws or rules are left as (or treated as) broad and simple. The process in both areas is never-ending: the kinds of reason that justified complications that were already introduced can always justify further complications. Thus, both in the law and in systems of moral rules, there always will be some cases for which the law or rules work admirably and some cases for which the law or rules seem less satisfactory. What do we say about cases of the latter sort?

One line of interpretation is as follows. In the law there are what H.L.A. Hart has termed 'recognised heads of exception', so that what might at first seem the implications of a law can be waived in a case in which, for example, a contract has been obtained under duress, or as a result of misleading representations, or would reward someone for an illegal activity, etc. Clearly also there is some judicial latitude in interpreting whether a given case falls under a 'recognised head of exception'. Yet it is far from clear that this latitude is unlimited. If, for example, I foolishly sign a contract the workings of which would seem to most people to be unfair, and which impoverishes my family and me and directly leads to misery for many others, and which benefits one, already wealthy, individual, there may be legal grounds for setting aside the contract; but one cannot be sure in advance that there will be.

Legally correct results, in this view, are a function of recognised procedures in a way in which morally correct results do not have to be. In morality, both before and after argument, it is logically possible to give weight to one's 'intuitive' sense that a certain action just is wrong, in a way that is not possible in the law. Rules of evidence have a role in the law that has no counterpart in morality. The law can achieve the important goals for which it was designed only if what is legally right is a function of the apparatus of statutes, rules, precedents, and recognised procedures. It is important that we can rely on this apparatus, and to a considerable degree anticipate its workings in advance. But one result is that, in cases in which it does not yield what intuitively seem to be good results, we are also trapped within the apparatus in a way in which, in morality, we are not trapped within the apparatus of moral rules and standard interpretations of rules.

A second line of interpretation in effect denies much of this. Moral considerations, in this view, can enter directly into the law, and in 'hard cases' especially they may well be decisive. Recognised procedures in the law allow considerable latitude in the use and interpretation of precedents, so that legal creativity ought to make possible, in any case, the outcome that intuitively seems right to all of us.

In this second line of interpretation there is much more similarity and overlap between law and morality than the first line indicates. But neither points to anything like an identity. We can see this if we examine the possibility, left open by both lines of interpretation, of a conscientious person, who has a generalised respect for law, encountering a case in which she or he judges that what the law commands is not for the best. This could happen within a system of law that is not very well devised; even passably good systems contain bad laws. Or it could be an instance in which the judiciary has blundered and appeals are exhausted. Without entering the controversy as to whether it is ever justified to disobey a law if one wishes to maintain respect for the system of laws that includes it, we can maintain that the positive position is not nonsensical. That is, it can be maintained without absurdity that, in some of the cases in which what the law commands is not for the best, the discrepancy justifies disobeying the law. Someone who says 'X is legally wrong but all things considered you ought to do X' may be right or wrong, but in any case is not talking nonsense. It is nonsense, however, to say 'X is morally wrong, but all things considered you ought to do X'.

Here we get at an important difference between morality and the law, a difference that can be put by saying that moral judgements in particular cases have conclusive prescriptivity and legal judgements do not. Whatever other differences there are, in terms of the importance of recognised procedures, rules of evidence, and the like, are related to this one: the tighter relation in the law between what counts as a proper decision and what counts as a proper process of reaching the decision is allied to a greater looseness in the connection between what counts as a proper decision and what finally an individual should do. Because of this, it is potentially misleading to regard morality simply as a de-institutionalised and shadowy form of law, or to regard the law simply as an institutionalised counterpart of morality.

Nevertheless, we have given reasons for thinking that there are some parallels between morality and law. One important parallel has not yet been mentioned. In certain societies, including the one in which Kant grew up and perhaps even our own, respect for the law is an important part of both childhood education and the entrenched attitudes of most adults. One almost instinctively obeys laws, and draws back from violating them; even someone who believes firmly in the validity of civil disobedience can at the same time feel that disobeying a law should not be something that one does lightly. All of the reasons that were given earlier for teaching moral rules to the young are also reasons for instilling a comparable respect for moral rules. (In neither the case of law nor of morality should the respect be so deep as to preclude thoughtful questioning.) If this is done, then moral rules will be felt as being very much like laws, with both the same generality and the same kind of authority. Unlike laws, however, moral rules do not have a formal apparatus of interpretation and enforcement. Some of the sanctions against violators are external, in the form of condemnation by others; but guilt is an important sanction, especially in cases in which a moral transgression can be kept secret. Furthermore, the origin of laws, unless one is oneself a member of the legislature, can seem entirely external. The morality that one learns as a child also has been devised without one's help, but one is asked to agree, to join in condemning certain kinds of conduct, in a way that finds no close parallel with regard to the law. People who join in condemning the moral transgressions of others, or the moral transgressions that they themselves might have committed but have managed to avoid, can very well have a sense that they are legislators of the law-like moral rules that they are maintaining. Because of this, especially, morality can feel very much like inner law that one imposes on oneself.

One must finally say that morality is morality rather than anything else. But what is unique can still be understood better by tracing similarities. The respects in which morality is law, and can be felt as law, help to illumine the way in which morality functions.

NOTES AND REFERENCES

Throughout I use the phrase 'moral rules' for generalisations thought to be usually or always morally binding. This is an established usage among philosophers, but there is room to question whether moral rules are strictly speaking rules at all. For the negative case, see G.J. Warnock, *The Object of Morality* (London, 1971), Chapters 4 and 5.

When I speak of Kant as offering three formulations of the categorical imperative, this reproduces Kant's count. (See the *Foundations of the Metaphysics of Morals*, Beck's translation, pp. 54 ff.) However, Kant produces variations on what essentially (for our purposes, and probably for his) remains the same formulation of the categorical imperative, so that it is possible, treating the variations as separate, to count as many as six formulations. For a general discussion, see Bruce Aune, *Kant's Theory of Morality* (Princeton, 1979).

The case that Kant was not a rigorist is presented very clearly by H.J. Paton in 'An alleged right to lie: a problem in Kantian ethics' (*Kant Studien*, 1953–4). Alan Donagan's defence of 'common morality' is contained in his *The Theory of Morality* (Chicago, 1977); his view of promising is stated on pp. 92–3. Wittgenstein's example of teaching children a game is to be found in *Philosophical Investigations*, trans. G.E.M. Anscombe (New York, 1953), p. 33. An entirely adequate moral code was promised by Richard Brandt in 'Toward a credible form of utilitarianism', in H.-N. Castaneda and G.

Naknikian (eds), *Morality and the Language of Conduct* (Detroit, 1963). Aristotle's discussion of the mean is to be found in *Nicomachean Ethics*, Book Two. His comment on adultery is in 1107a (p. 44 of the Bobbs-Merrill edition of the translation by M. Ostwald).

A good discussion of the way in which moral notions structure perception is to be found in Julius Kovesi's *Moral Notions* (London, 1967). William Kneale has related the origins of morality to law in his 'Objectivity in morals' (*Philosophy*, 1950). H.L.A. Hart's comment about 'recognised heads of exception' in the law comes from his 'The ascription of responsibility and rights', in A. Flew (ed.), *Logic and Language*, First Series (New York, 1965), p. 154. My own inclination is entirely to accept Hart's general account of the law. For a different view, see Ronald Dworkin, *Taking Rights Seriously* (Cambridge, Mass., 1977). I am indebted to conversations with Dr Lynda Sharp Paine, which led me to modify the first version of my discussion of the relation between morality and the law; she is not responsible for what remains. Finally, I should express my great debt to the treatment of moral generalisations to be found in R.M. Hare's 'Ethical theory and utilitarianism', in H.D. Lewis (ed.), *Contemporary British Philosophy*, Fourth Series (London, 1976).

Chapter 3

Morality as Interpersonally Neutral

Morality, like the law, applies 'irrespective of persons'. In modern legal codes there cannot be laws on the order of 'Such and such, which generally speaking is a criminal act, is permitted to J.W. Bloggs'. Neither can there be genuine moral generalisations qualified for individuals on the order of 'Such and such, which generally speaking is morally wrong, is morally acceptable if performed by J.W. Bloggs'. Having said this, we should quickly add that people are, in their roles as presidents, wives, mothers, executors of estates, etc., legally and morally allowed to do some things which would be condemned in others. Plainly the interpersonal neutrality of morality is a more com- plicated and qualified fact than it might first be thought to be.

The simplest way of presenting the interpersonal neutrality of morality is to say that no proper name can occur in moral rules. But this may be both too weak and too technical: too weak, because as we shall see a stronger claim of interpersonal neutrality is justified, and too technical because what matters after all is not how sentences are to be formed, but what is permitted. At the other extreme, one might say with Kant (in his first formulation of the categorical imperative) that nothing is right for one person which would not be right as a universal practice. But, as it stands, this sounds too strong a claim. Kant I think almost certainly would have permitted us to make allowances, under the rubric of the categorical imperative, for people's special roles and positions: this would yield maxims on the order of 'If one is in the role of X, it is right to do Y'. But what if what is crucial is not one's formal role (as president, wife, mother, etc.) but rather one's special needs or abilities? In principle there is no reason why, again under the rubric of the categorical imperative, we could not have a maxim which said 'Someone with special needs or abilities X is justified in doing Y'. But now we almost certainly have gone beyond what Kant would have tolerated, and it is also not clear what kind of interpersonal neutrality we are left with.

Let us begin with the logical core of interpersonal neutrality. The principle of universalisability, developed and argued for by R.M. Hare, most notably in *Freedom and Reason*, states that nothing is right, wrong, good, or bad for X unless it is also right, wrong, good, or bad for anyone else in relevantly similar circumstances. Hare argues that this is a logical truth, rather than a substantive moral principle, and that in this sense it is morally neutral (although he also shows in some detail that it is morally useful). Let me say that I find Hare's arguments on all of these points to be entirely convincing.

As it stands, this principle does not imply that nothing can be right for me that would not also be right for anyone else. It may be that there are relevant differences between my situation and other people's situations, or indeed between my tastes, interests, needs, or abilities and other people's. There is what amounts to a burden of proof as regards what counts as relevant differences: in the general run of cases it is very difficult to make out that, for example, hair colour is a relevant difference that would justify a moral choice for one agent that would not be justified for another. Skin colour and racial origin also are difficult to make out as relevant differences in relation to moral decisions. Also one can always ask a bigot to imagine what it would be like if he turned out to have a black or Jewish ancestor, or if he woke up with a different skin colour: should he then be treated in the way he now advocates treating others? This argument can be persuasive (within the limits of the sensitivity and power of imagination normally to be found in bigots). However, a true fanatic can answer 'Yes'. However morally repugnant bigotry is, there is no purely logical flaw in advocating that people of different race or skin colour be treated differently, as long as one would apply the same judgements to oneself if one were of that race or skin colour.

The logical requirement of universalisability thus carries us very little towards interpersonal neutrality. A proper consideration of the function of morality carries us further. Morality as a social device must make a general appeal to members of society. Inherent in moral judgement, as David Hume pointed out, is the sense that the judgement should be shared: that others, from their perspective, should see roughly what one sees from one's own perspective. This distinguishes moral judgements from judgements purely of self-interest. To say 'Bloggs is doing something that harms my interests' is not to launch an appeal for the agreement and support of others in the way that one does in saying 'Bloggs is treating me unfairly (or is behaving in an immoral way)'. It goes without saying that appeals can be unsuccessful: someone can have moral views which finally no one shares. But for them to be moral views there must be the sense that they *should* be shared.

To say that this is inherent in the function of morality is not to say that all moralities fulfil this function equally well. One could without logical contradiction have a morality that preferred the interests of a master race and that stipulated that other races should know their place. Such a morality would be deficient, but might, at least for a time, be viable. Even then, it is hard to imagine that it would be viable for long unless *some* core rules were applied equally to members of all races. If what we call murder and theft were permitted to members of the master race and to no others, it is hard to believe that the appeal of the moral code would not be limited.

This leads us to the following point. A morality can function well in its social role only if it can appeal effectively to a wide range of people in a society. In practice this means that the functioning of the morality must be able to be perceived as in the general interest, rather than merely the interests of a particular class or group. Furthermore, a morality will more effectively have general appeal if it can be regarded as making roughly equal demands on all. If some people seem to escape the demands of morality almost entirely, there may well be a sense that morality functions for their benefit more than for the general benefit. In any case, envy may suggest to others that they, too, could have light demands made of them by morality. Thus, all things equal, a morality that allows people to claim that they are special cases in relation to core requirements can be expected to function less effectively than a morality that does not allow this. These are substantive rather than logical points, concerning in very general terms which moralities might function more effectively than others. But it also helps to explain why it is no accident that viable moralities pretty generally have core requirements (governing such matters as murder, theft, torture, and promise-keeping) which apply irrespective of persons.

This provides us with the beginning of an argument that goes some of the distance between Hare's universalisability principle and Kant's first formulation of the categorical imperative. Hare's universalisability principle is logically valid, and specifies a minimal neutrality to be found in any consistent set of moral judgements. It leaves open the logical possibility that there could be significant relevant differences between persons so that the moral requirements for one person could differ significantly from those for others. Kant's first formulation of the categorical imperative (interpreted as implying that rules should apply irrespective of persons) is not logically valid. He cannot prove *a priori* that there are not special features of Bloggs that make his stealing an entirely different matter from (and hence more justified than) any of us stealing. On the other hand, our sense of how a moral system ought to function suggests that any moral system which left a loophole for Bloggs in a matter as central as this would be deficient; and in this respect Kant's first formulation of the categorical imperative appeals to our sense of what morality ought to be.

All of this suggests that an effective and viable morality will place high priority on an understanding that core requirements apply irrespective of persons. Kant's first formulation of the categorical imperative captures this neatly. On the other hand, it is a little too neat. First of all, high priority is not the same as absolute priority; even a highly effective and viable morality can recognise cases in which personal needs of an unusual sort create exceptions to core requirements. Secondly, morality consists of more than just its core. Even if we are very highly reluctant to grant exceptions to people in matters of killing, stealing, breaking promises, etc., there may be moral decisions of other sorts in which we would be more willing to consider relevant the needs, abilities, tastes, or interests of the person who is making the decision. All of this needs to be spelled out.

We have already pointed out that most thoughtful people would agree that generally valid moral rules can have exceptions. At the same time, we have seen that admitting an exception to a rule within the core of morality damages the system, by making the morality that much less effective and viable. This is a cost which must always be weighed against whatever is gained by admitting the exception. The cost, though, can vary with the nature of the exception. If it is suggested that it is morally right for someone to break a core rule because that person has an extraordinarily strong desire to do what is prohibited by the rule, that is to suggest something the cost of which would be prohibitive. If a general sense develops that keen desires confer special moral freedom, more and more people will fancy their desires to be keen, and others are likely to be envious enough to come to resent the demands of morality on them. A similarly prohibitive cost would be involved if core requirements of morality were waived for someone on the grounds of extraordinary abilities. The cost would be almost as great if the excuse is need: if we judge that people are free to break promises simply because they are in a tight spot, or to steal simply because they are poor, the effectiveness of these moral rules is very likely to diminish. Those in slightly tight spots or whose incomes are not as high as they would like may well pass from envy to the sense that they too deserve to be exceptions. On the other hand, there can be extreme and specific cases for which the costs are less. In the well-known case of the man who steals some over-priced medicine for his dying wife which he could not obtain in any other way, if we should agree that the man is justified in stealing it is not at all likely that others will be envious and thereby resent more the demands of morality on themselves, nor is it likely that there will be many people who will claim that their cases are the same. A reasonable person will not morally judge cases like this without knowing a great deal both about the details and about the possible alternatives; what I wish to point out is merely that a morality that allowed exceptions in some such cases could yet remain highly effective and viable.

There are moral decisions also that seem to most people to lie less close to the core, and in part because of this can seem more personal. A contemporary example is the decision of whether or not to get a divorce. Some readers may balk at labelling this a moral decision, on the grounds that it is too personal, and not at all the business of society. But in some cases the possibilities of serious harm, to the spouse of the person initiating the divorce or to children, are real and obvious enough, and the alternatives stark and dramatic enough, so that a reflective person might well consider the decision a moral one, even if after reflection she or he decided that a divorce was justified. A similar moral problem concerns Gauguin's decision to desert his family in order to paint in the South Seas. Divorce and desertion are just two of the acts by which a person can affect the happiness of those close to her or him, and we pointed out in the last chapter that many of these acts are not commonly brought within the purview of morality. But because what is done is more drastic and visible, and because it can be viewed as a matter of a single willed decision, rather than hundreds of thought-less daily decisions, divorce and desertion do seem to be matters for moral judgement. Another example of a moral decision away from the core might be the well-known one used by Sartre, of the pupil who is considering whether to leave his mother (who depends on him) in order to fight for his country with the Free French in the Second World War. This again looks like a moral choice, not only because serious general demands are at stake (loyalty to a parent, loyalty to one's country), but also because there are possibilities of serious and visible good or harm for others coming out of the young man's choice.

In any case like these, it would be foolish for someone making a decision to ignore totally her or his own needs and desires. That is not to say that these should automatically be decisive. It may be that there are certain kinds of likely damage to a spouse and children such that no needs or desires of someone contemplating a divorce would outweigh them. Abilities also can be relevant without necessarily being decisive. One may wonder whether Gauguin was justified in leaving his family in order to paint in the South Seas, but whether it is adequate or not there is some justification; if Gauguin had been a mediocre artist the justification for his choice would have been poorer. Even if Gauguin and Sartre's pupil had the same core requirements as the rest of us, not to steal, torture or kill, not to inflict needless pain and to save lives when possible, it may be that there are some moral decisions for which needs, desires, and abilities would make different choices more appro-priate for them than us. An effective and viable morality can allow this.

Thus the first formulation of Kant's categorical imperative appears more plausible as a statement of what must be true (or at least approximately true) of the core of an effective and viable morality than it is in relation to Gauguin's or Sartre's pupil's choice. Having said this, we must admit that we are in an area of moral controversy. Many people will want to insist, as Kant certainly would have insisted, that there are no personal exceptions to moral demands, that if it is wrong for Bloggs to desert his family in order to paint in the South Seas it was wrong for Gauguin. We can feel the pull of this: one hesitates to give Gauguin licence to do anything that would be wrong for Bloggs. But finally the cases are not the same. One can say this without taking sides on what Gauguin should have done. And the general functioning of morality is not threatened if we say that Gauguin might have been right to leave his family in the way in which it is threatened if we say that Gauguin could be justified in torturing others or in refusing to save lives.

Thus far we have considered the claims of Kant's first formulation of the categorical imperative. Kant considered his three formulations to be just three alternative ways of putting the same requirement. But the second formulation, interpreted as a principle of respect for persons, has been emphasised especially by a number of recent writers. Therefore we should now ask what the meaning of respect for persons is, and what its moral implications are.

Kant himself appears to have had at least two things in mind in his second formulation of the categorical imperative. One is the familiar notion of not harming, exploiting, or ignoring the interests of, other persons: not treating them merely as instruments or obstacles to be dealt with in our pursuit of our own goals. The other is deference to the moral autonomy, and possible goodness, of others. As the third formulation stresses, we should maintain our standards of behaviour towards others as if their standards are high, whatever the likely truth about them. But also we cannot lie or break promises to others 'for their own good'; we must treat them as responsible moral agents who can make their own decisions. Respect for persons thus enjoins not only concern for others' welfare but also respect for their inherent dignity as rational beings.

This is an admirable ideal, and any decent person must feel the force of its appeal. It was also a radical ideal for its time, and perhaps for ours. Kant, the great admirer of Rousseau, stresses a moral requirement which is opaque to those preoccupied with class or intellectual superiority or with the superior craft of bureaucratic managers.

But what are its implications? If Kant is to be believed, they are exactly the implications of the first and third formulations of the categorical imperative. Respect for persons thus turns out to under-write a code of rules that enjoins us not to murder, steal, lie, break promises, etc. We have already discussed the strengths and limitations of such a moral system.

It is possible to take respect for persons further. Two ways in which it can be extended deserve especial notice. One is that in all decisions that affect the welfare of other persons (or, in a more qualified version, in all moral decisions that affect the welfare of other persons) one should weigh everyone's welfare (including one's own) equally. In this extension the principle of respect for persons begins to sound like a utilitarian principle. The other way of extending the principle is that one can take it as forbidding anything which diminishes the autonomy (or neglects the consent) of others or of oneself. Thus the principle could be taken as an endorsement of non-manipulative personal relations or of participatory democracy or (as it has been by Robert Paul Wolff) of a kind of anarchism. Alternatively, the Kantian tradition can be held to underwrite the requirement that there be no distribution of wealth and power that would not have been agreed to by everyone, had everyone been ignorant of what his or her actual position in society would be.

There is no space to comment in detail on all of these Kantian outbuildings. A general comment can be made on the second line of development. Autonomy or consent is clearly worthy of respect, and at least one writer in the utilitarian tradition (Jonathan Glover) has argued that autonomy must be taken as a good. We can agree that there are strong reasons for maintaining a generalised respect for autonomy; later in the book the weight and function of this will be discussed. But this is not to say that considerations of autonomy must in every case be decisive. Should, for example, no one be required to contribute to any governmental project to which she or he has not consented? The good work left undone, and the possibilities of societal disintegration, make an anarchist response extremely unappealing to most of us. If taxation violates autonomy (as at least in a few cases it is plausible to say it does), then it appears that sometimes it is justifiable to violate autonomy. We are left with the result that considerations of autonomy must be weighed against other considerations, in which case respect for autonomy does not by itself provide solutions to a full range of moral problems.

The first line of development leads to different difficulties which are largely difficulties associated with deciding how utilitarianism is to be formulated or applied. They too will be discussed later. One element, though, deserves discussion now. This is the emphasis on equal consideration. The equality points in two directions. On one hand, others should be given the same consideration (at least in moral decisions) as oneself: this is a prohibition of selfishness. On the other hand, others we detest or think very little of should be given the same consideration as others we love or think very highly of.

There is something very appealing in this, and it captures some of the spirit of Kant's third formulation of the categorical imperative. There are areas of conduct in which something like this does seem to govern our moral judgements. In decisions involving what we would normally call property rights, for example, we do not feel entitled to feather our nests at the expense of others, or to benefit our children at the expense of strangers, or to make off with the property of those we loathe and give it to those we love. On the other hand, most people earn money primarily in order to benefit themselves and their families rather than strangers. In virtually every area of private life it is normally considered acceptable to favour one's own interests and the interests of those one loves over the interests of strangers.

One way of taking account of this is to say that a principle of equal consideration governs moral choices but not non-moral choices. One is impartial, let us say, in one's decisions as a banker, or as someone considering applicants for a job; but impartiality of this sort is out of place for someone giving gifts or deciding with whom to spend leisure time. There is a (perhaps apocryphal) story of a utilitarian who was troubled by the partiality involved in his paying for his children's education, when the money might have done more good elsewhere. But many people might think this is importing into a personal, non-moral area of life questions and standards that are appropriate only in relation to moral choice.

Comfortable as the division between moral and non-moral areas of life is, it may be too comfortable, for reasons that will be discussed later in the book. Also, it will not help us to arrive at a simple view of the requirement of equal consideration. Andrew Oldenquist has pointed out that there are moral choices with regard to which we normally do not think it appropriate to exercise equal consideration. If two children are drowning nearby, and there is time to save only one, most of us would consider it perfectly appropriate to save one's own child rather than a stranger. The decision clearly is a moral one, and impartiality seems not entirely in place.

Even here we are under constraints. It might be right to save one's child's life in preference to another's, but wrong to save one's child from being injured rather than save another child from being killed. It looks as if most of us would consider it proper to prefer our own interests or those of our loved ones in some kinds of moral choices, but not in others, and as if the degree of preference might vary with the kind of case. We shall explore these topics further in Chapter 11. But enough has been said for it to be clear that a principle of equal consideration, like a principle of respect for autonomy, does not by itself directly solve the full range of moral problems to which it might be applied.

In any case, almost all of the extensions of Kant's second formulation of the categorical imperative are ideologically suffused. It is as if they catch a latent radicalism of which Kant himself, despite the portrait of Rousseau adorning his study, was only partially aware. Two ideological currents should be mentioned, which affect many people's views of the proper role of principles of equal consideration or of generalised respect for autonomy of persons.

First there is what might be called the elitist current. It is sometimes believed, to put it baldly, that some people are worth more than others. This is a view held in both respectable and contemptible versions. Those who hold that racial origin and skin colour can make one person worth more than another are rather easily dismissed. Those who consider educational qualifications the decisive factor also might be dismissed as taking a rather narrow view of what makes human life worthwhile. But someone in the tradition of G.E. Moore, who holds that some experiences are more worthwhile than others, and furthermore believes that some people have an ability or a knack for having worthwhile experiences and that some other people have not, cannot so easily be dismissed. Whatever one thinks of this kind of elitism, it is not grotesque or inhuman. And this leaves open the question of whether, in some respects, there are people who deserve better than equal consideration.

Having said all this, one must add that there is ample room for doubt as to how far it leads. First of all, the difficulty of arriving at any unbiased judgement of which sorts of people have more worthwhile experiences is so great that one might well decide, for all or almost all practical, moral, and public policy purposes, to treat all people as equally deserving. There are so many unpleasant repercussions of unequal treatment (vanity on the part of those who get better than equal treatment, and envy on the part of those who get worse than equal treatment) that one might decide on these grounds also that equal treatment is the best policy even if some version of elitism is correct.

The second ideological current flows in the direction of equality: absolute equality in moral and political respects, and more equality in matters of wealth and power. Some egalitarians might hold it unjustified to treat the cases of Gauguin and Bloggs, who desert their families in order to paint in the South Seas, differently. But the major direction of this current, of course, is towards a reconstruction of human societies which is thought of as a moral requirement. It is morally unjustifiable, in this view, that some people should be privileged, in certain respects, in relation to other people. The kinds of privileges under attack can vary. They can involve higher income, or superior medical care, or superior educational opportunity, or superior opportunities for leisure enjoyment. The attack in each case is that it is morally unacceptable for such privileges to exist.

This raises an important point with regard to the interpretation of morality's interpersonal neutrality. Traditionally this interpersonal neutrality has been placed against the backdrop of a social and political order, so that what interpersonal neutrality required was that, *given* the existing social and political order, or something like it, one fulfil one's obligations irrespective of persons. Given existing property arrangements, for example, one was required to follow the same policy concerning theft with regard to everyone, including people one loved, people one loathed, the wealthy, the not so wealthy, etc. It can be argued that this working out of interpersonal neutrality against the backdrop of the existing social and political order is in fact not neutral: that it contains a bias in favour of those who benefit most from the *status quo*. Interpersonal neutrality, in this view, extends to issues of the possible reconstruction of society.

This leads us back to the claim that certain kinds of privilege are morally unjustifiable. Some would say that disparities in medical care are not morally justifiable, but that differences in income (within certain limits) are. Some who advocate equality of educational opportunity hold that this implies that comparable facilities and attention be available to all; others support a stronger interpretation, that true educational equality requires compensation in the form of better facilities and more attention for those initially less able. One scarcely need say that there are a large number of possible views as to just what kinds of privilege or advantage are morally unjustifiable.

These are moral issues, but they are also political and ideological issues. Rather than place myself on a political and ideological spectrum, let me just make two points. One is that the complexity of the issues is such that it would be wrong to claim that there is one possible answer that straightforwardly follows from the notion of equal consideration. John Rawls has made an ingenious and complex attempt to base his views on the notion of equal consent of designers of a society who are placed in an 'original position' in which they do not know what their roles in the society will be. However, he does not explain why some of these designers of society might not be inclined to gamble: a social arrangement in which many people would be much better off than in the society he favours, and the worse-off members of society only slightly worse off, might represent a very appealing gamble. What Rawls does convey and defend very well, though, is the sense that very many people have nowadays that there are degrees of inequality that are morally indefensible. Just how one draws the line between what is morally defensible and what is morally indefensible may well be one of those issues about which reasonable people can differ, but there is a widespread sense that any social order which includes really abject and grinding poverty side by side with great wealth is morally indefensible.

This leads me to the second point, which is that the terms of discussions such as this one rapidly change. They would have been different a hundred or two hundred years ago, and may well be different again a hundred or two hundred years from now. Our attitudes towards, say, people who because of inherited wealth do not work have changed a great deal; and attitudes towards people who, as a result of work, enjoy a great deal more wealth than those around them may change similarly. Of course we cannot predict the development of moral attitudes with anything like certainty, and in any case we should not assume that the flow of moral opinion is necessarily in the right direction. But there is room for caution in what one takes as obvious, and ample warning against complacency about received moral views.

Let me summarise the view of the interpersonal neutrality of morality that has emerged in this chapter. Logic requires us to impose the same moral requirements on any one human being as on all others, unless there are relevant differences between one person and others that justify different moral judgements. Of course there always are *some* differences; but reasonable people are generally prepared to dismiss out of hand any claim that differences in hair or skin colour, racial origin, taste in foods, etc., justify different moral requirements, or indeed different sets of rights. Whether differences in intelligence, ability, sensitivity, or refinement justify different moral requirements may seem to some people more problematic. The cases of Gauguin and of Bloggs, a mediocre artist who also deserts his family in order to paint in the South Seas, might give us pause. The view that behaviour which is justified for Gauguin would be morally unjustified for Bloggs may be, in the end, wrong; but it does not seem absurd, or able to be dismissed out of hand. It may lead us to wonder whether there is any interpersonal neutrality in morality beyond the logical requirement of the universalisability principle.

Beyond the minimal-seeming logical requirement that the universalisability principle imposes, there is also a functional requirement of interpersonal neutrality. In order for a morality to function effectively over the long run, it must be perceived as not making appreciably heavier or lighter demands on anyone. Heavier demands lead to resentment; lighter demands lead to envy. This functional requirement, rather than any purely logical point, appears to be at the root of Kant's first formulation of the categorical imperative. We assume, as a general rule, that in any properly functioning morality what is required of us will be required of everyone else, and that what is permitted to us will be permitted to everyone else.

My claim is that this functional requirement of interpersonal neutrality is not as tight and neat as Kant thought. It certainly applies to what I have called the core of morality, which includes the moral rules we learn as children. If we allow that there are no exceptions to the rules against stealing or breaking promises, for example, it is only in cases with remarkable circumstances apart from the character, personality, or abilities of the agent: we would not license someone to steal or to break promises merely on the ground that he or she was a remarkable individual. There is an area of moral judgement, however, in which facts about the desires, needs, and abilities of the person making a decision are morally relevant: decisions about divorce or of whether to leave a dependent parent in order to fight with the Free French are of this character. A morality can function effectively even if it allows for morally relevant differences among individuals in this area.

Finally, it may be said that the function of a morality is not only to regulate certain sorts of conduct but also to underwrite (or undermine) a social order: questions of the design of society cannot be separated from morality. This leaves room for the following claim. The functional requirement for a morality to be effective in the long run is not only that core requirements apply equally to all, but also that the morality requires social arrangements to which all people reasonably would consent. Just as a morality may well lose its hold on people who believe that it requires more of them than others, so also it may lose its hold on people who take it to underwrite an unacceptably inferior position for them. Interpersonal neutrality, in this view, points toward greater social equality.

One can concede this general point without arriving at any precise view of just what social, economic, or political inequalities are morally unacceptable. It may be helpful in this regard to think of morality on the model of social engineering rather than social mathematics: what we must determine is the tolerances of a system, rather than a single precise solution to a problem. We have seen that interpersonal neutrality does not require anything as neat as what Kant suggests: an effective morality can tolerate some kinds of differential treatment of persons, away from the core. In the same way, an effective morality can tolerate some degree of social and economic inequality among persons with different degrees of ability or intelligence or with different work habits, although in the long run it may not be able to tolerate either the social and economic inequalities that were common a hundred years ago or even those that are common now. A more egalitarian position than this suggests does not appear to have either logical or functional justification.

NOTES AND REFERENCES

A good general discussion of universalisability is provided by J.L. Mackie in *Ethics: Inventing Right and Wrong* (Harmondsworth, 1977) Chapter 4. David Hume's point about the appeal to the agreement of others that is inherent in moral judgement can be found in his *Enquiry Concerning the Principles of Morals*, Section IX, Part I, para. 6. Sartre's example of the pupil who must choose whether to join the Free French or stay with his dependent mother is found in his 'Existentialism is a humanism', in W. Kaufmann (ed.), *Existentialism* (London, 1957). It should be mentioned in passing that the views expressed in this popular lecture are on the whole not representative of Sartre's philosophy, either then or later. Kant's admiration for Rousseau is discussed in Ernst Cassirer's *Rousseau, Kant, Goethe* (Hamden, Conn. 1961).
Robert Paul Wolff's Kantian anarchism is argued for in his *In Defense of Anarchism*

(New York, 1970). John Rawls has discussed social and economic justice within a broadly Kantian tradition in his *A Theory of Justice* (Cambridge, Mass., 1971). Jonathan Glover argues that autonomy must be taken as a good in his *Causing Death and Saving Lives* (Harmondsworth, 1977), pp. 73–4. The example of the two children drowning, and the general point that it makes, are taken from an unpublished manuscript of Andrew Oldenquist's, 'Universalizability and the self'.

Part Two
The Need for Ethical Theory

Chapter 4

The Nature of Ethical Theory

Thus far we have provided a highly interpreted description of what almost everyone in our society would recognise as morality. Some of the interpretations may be controversial: diehard Kantians might feel, for example, that more credit should be given to the categorical imperative as a moral tool, and some people might be disturbed at our pessimism about the prospects for rigorism. But on the whole we have stayed close to the phenomena. What we have described, in other words, is the morality of ordinary people, and not of philosophers holding some special ethical view. Furthermore, the morality that we described does, at least to a considerable degree, work. It tells millions of people, quickly and efficiently, not to murder, steal, torture, break their promises, etc.; people very often follow its guidance, and have an added sense of security in the thought that other people also often follow its guidance.

It is worth asking then whether anything more is needed. This part of the book is entitled 'The Need for Ethical Theory'; but the reader may well doubt, as I once doubted, whether in fact there is any need for ethical theory. An argument to this effect goes as follows. The obvious analogue to ethical theory is scientific theory. However, scientific theory fills a need which simply does not exist in the same way in ethics. First of all, the primary goal of the sciences is to explain; and we need scientific theories to explain the facts before us. The primary goal of ethics surely has something to do with promoting good conduct, and good conduct appears to be readily available without any aid from theory. Furthermore, scientific theories enable us to make predictions, and also lead to useful technological developments; neither of these achievements could be attributed to ethical theory. Thus it is far from clear that ethical theory contributes to any worthwhile goal.

In what follows I shall argue that there is a need for ethical theory, and that ethical theory can contribute to important goals. The argument will refer repeatedly back to loose ends and gaps in morality that were revealed in the first section. First, however, we must have a clear picture of what is being argued for. We must begin with a characterisation of what ethical theory is.

This in turn must be based on the recognition that an ethical theory may do more than one kind of thing. One thing that anything that would be called an ethical theory must do is to provide a decision procedure, either for all choices or for moral choices only. This decision procedure must in some way go beyond or supplement familiar rules of conduct: something that merely told one not to murder, steal, etc., would scarcely qualify as a theory. What Kant provides, with his apparatus for testing maxims of conduct, an apparatus which presumably could be used in relation to unfamiliar as well as familiar maxims, does go beyond and supplement familiar moral rules. So does classical utilitarianism.

Anything that would be called an ethical theory must also provide a way of understanding obligation: a theory, that is, must be a system of interpretation as well as an apparatus for making decisions. Kant not only provides a fundamental test of moral maxims but also provides a way of making sense of familiar moral rules, so that these are seen as somehow requirements of rationality rather than as commands by God or by the leaders of society or as special and unfounded requirements of life itself. The classical utilitarians interpreted the familiar moral requirements as devices to maximise happiness. No doubt there are many other ways in which an ethical theory could interpret the demands of traditional morality while on the whole accepting traditional moral rules. It is sometimes said, because of all this, that the difference between, say, Kant and the utilitarians lies more in how they view our obligations than in how they would have us act. As we shall see, this is a half-truth; but it is a useful half-truth when juxtaposed with the simple-minded view that the meaning of any ethical theory is simply its results for conduct.

If what I have just said is correct, then a description of how morality functions which is itself neutral between ethical theories is impossible; and this conclusion applies to the account given in Part One of this book. This must be granted, along with the further point that the interpretations that were given have a bit more in common with the utilitarians than with Kant, although they completely agree with neither. However, two other things should be pointed out. One is that the interpretations earlier provided were argued, so that they are not in this sense question-begging and there are grounds for thinking them better than rival interpretations. There is no reason, after all, to think that all ethical theories are of equal merit.

Secondly, it should be clear by now that the average person's view of morality is by no means as innocent of anything like theory as one might assume. Even someone who has never heard of Kant, let alone read him, may have acquired the idea that moral decisions must be decisions of principle. Part of my argument in Part One was that to a large extent Kant can be seen as distilling and putting into a theoretical form assumptions about morality that were already embedded in our culture; and it may be that his philosophy, in turn, has had indirect cultural effects that have slightly strengthened these assumptions (or that have prevented them from being weakened more than they have been). The interpretations the average person gives to morality may, of course, not be entirely consistent, and they are unlikely to be very much thought out. This in itself suggests an argument, beyond the ones that will be supplied, that ethical theory is needed: the alternatives are not ethical theory and no theory at all, but instead good theory on one hand and bad and fuzzy theory on the other.

Any ethical theory must provide a decision procedure that goes beyond or supplements familiar rules of conduct, and must provide a way of understanding obligation. There are other things that theories may do. Some theories provide a way of assessing moral agents. A morality can function only if, in a wide range of cases, people know what is expected of them: that is, which acts are acceptable and which are unacceptable. This is essential; but it is natural, after we have finished praising and condemning actions, to praise and condemn individuals as well. An ethical theory can thus provide a way of judging who is a good person and who is a bad person, as well as a decision procedure for actions. This is a peripheral rather than a central function of ethical theory. Classical utilitarianism has it hardly at all, although certainly the materials are there for someone who wishes to construct a utilitarian view of the moral worth of individuals. Kant is more concerned than the utilitarians with individual moral worth, but he cautions against assuming that people's motives (even one's own motives) are what they seem to be. Thus Kant's theory provides a determinate (within the limits earlier discussed) way of determining which moral maxims and which actions are acceptable, but not a determinate way of estimating the moral worth of individuals.

One need not, of course, subscribe to a highly developed ethical theory in order to have ways of estimating the moral worth of individuals (including one's own moral worth). This goes back to the earlier point that theory-like elements are present in the thinking of ordinary people. But it should be added that a multiplicity of theory-like elements, some of them pulling in opposite directions from one another, can be present in ordinary moral thought. This is pointed up very nicely in a well-known essay of Thomas Nagel's on 'moral luck'.

Nagel discusses four kinds of moral luck, only one of which concerns me here: luck in how one's actions and projects turn out. With regard to this, Nagel points out that there is a wide range of cases in which what we turn out to have done depends on factors not under our control, even though it is not true that we are not in control of our actions or are acting involuntarily. A simple example is the case in which we drive a bit too fast: the ultimate character of our action may depend on whether a child runs in front of our car in such a way that we cannot avoid hitting the child but could have avoided it if we had been driving at a normal speed. The ordinary idea of moral assessment is that people can be judged only on the basis of what they intended. But if only intentions matter then the cases of the reckless driver who hits the child and of the reckless driver for whom no child runs out are the same, and yet we find ourselves inclined to regard these two people differently. In one's own case, there seems a great difference between driving too fast and hitting a child and driving too fast and not hitting a child.

Nagel regards the phenomena of moral luck as 'undermining moral assessment', but they can equally be regarded as setting up tensions within the process of assessing personal merit or desert. The tensions caused by the moral luck involved in how one's actions and projects turn out can be placed in a broader context as follows. A relatively recent strain of thought, which owes something to Kant, and something perhaps to the New Testament and to Classical Greek thought, inclines us to raise or lower our estimate of merit or desert only on the basis of intentions. In this view, actual results do not matter: no one is responsible for what she or he does not intend, so that what is accidental does not count for or against one. One can be given credit or blame for what one intends, whether or not it comes to pass. This strain of thought is, as it were, very close to the surface in our thinking about merit or desert, so that it seems only 'rational'. There is in all of us, though, an older strain, very close to what Arthur Adkins has described as the thought about merit of Homeric Greece. In this strain of thought, strength and being able to achieve what is needed for oneself and one's dependants count for far more than do the more co-operative virtues, and results matter much more than intentions. As civilisation progressed, in Greece and elsewhere, this kind of thinking came under attack; but it never has disappeared. Even today people who behave virtuously but are weak and fail to solve their problems and the problems of those who depend on them are regularly viewed with contempt or condescension. Even today, in assessing ourselves and others, we take results of behaviour as seriously as we do our estimate of whether someone genuinely 'meant well'. Even in the extreme case, in which an action of mine, well intended and carried out with reasonable care and a moderate degree of skill, results in harm to someone which (given hindsight) might have been avoided, I am very likely to feel something with much the felt quality of guilt.

There are two separable issues between these two lines of thought about personal merit: the issue between judging merit on the basis of intentions only and judging with an eye to results, and the issue between assigning merit on the basis primarily of the co-operative virtues (the core of what we consider moral virtue) and taking into account a wider group of virtues. Let me say right away that I do not wish to defend the older view: on the whole the newer view was indeed a considerable advance. But it should be pointed out that there are facts which make the older view less 'irrational', and less easy entirely to dismiss, than it may at first seem. First, important as the co-operative virtues are, it would be one-sided to regard them as the sole grounds for esteem or disesteem. They can be prized without being prized exclusively. Our opinion of others can legitimately be affected by other factors, including their wit, charm, cleverness, general competence at practical matters, and even their speed at foot-races or the quality of their singing voices. Kant nowhere denies this, but in his famous praise of 'the good will' he tends to slight it.

Secondly, as has been widely recognised, there is always room for doubt as to what one's true motives or intentions were, or indeed whether one exercised due care and reasonable skill in carrying through an action. Ever since the advent of psychoanalysis we have become used to the idea that many accidents are not truly accidents. Nietzsche conveys a related thought in his remark that to be a person of character is to have one's typical experience. It is not totally irrational to suspect that some people make their luck; although it would be wrong to exaggerate this, or to think it true in every case.

The point, in any event, is that something like ethical theory is embedded in the average person's thinking about such matters as moral responsibility, merit, and desert, and that in fact conflicting and confused lines of thought are embedded. This will continue to be the case whether or not ethical philosophers interfere further; and, even if a philosopher succeeds in proposing a lustrous ethical theory which wins everyone's assent, it will continue to be true that other, conflicting, lines of thought will remain embedded in people's thinking about ethics. The most that ethical theory can accomplish, in this regard, is to increase clarity close to the surface.

It has become commonplace among philosophers of science that there is no 'neutral given': that the data upon which the sciences rest are themselves permeated with theoretical or theory-like elements. We can see that something similar must be true of the immediate sense that people have that a given action is allowable or immoral, or that a person is to be respected or is worthy of contempt. In ethics too there is no 'neutral given'. We need to examine this more closely, partly in relation to the problem of how an ethical theory can make good its claim to acceptance.

First of all, there is the well-known problem of whether there is anything at all in ethics which genuinely corresponds to data in the sciences. G.E. Moore in *Principia Ethica* used the word 'intuition' for self-evident judgements of value that might play that role; after some decades of scorn the term 'intuition' has undergone a curious revival, and philosophers frequently nowadays appeal to our 'intuitions' about what kinds of conduct are appropriate, about justice, and about values. But this renewed licensing of the word 'intuition' does not remove the problem of whether, indeed, there is anything at all in ethics that genuinely corresponds to data in the sciences.

What many philosophers speak of as intuitions appear dissimilar to scientific data in some obvious respects. First of all, they are not the results of a perceptual mechanism in the way that data of the sciences are. Anyone who wishes to mask this difference by speaking of a moral sense should be asked to locate it in the body. Secondly it is not plausible to construe immediate ethical judgements as referential in the way in which 'There is a blue light before me', or 'There is a loud noise nearby' are referential. G.E. Moore spoke of goodness as a non-natural quality; but this is to plug a real gap with a metaphysical invention, and will not work.

Because of all this, it is very tempting to say that there are referential constraints on the sciences but not on ethics. This is a tempting half-truth. We should look carefully to see what is true in it and what is not.

Philosophical accounts of the constraints on the sciences have been modified a great deal in recent years. Scientific theories used to be thought of as straightforwardly implying statements about what was or would be observed. Some of these statements, about observations of a kind that had not yet taken place, amounted to predictions. Scientists then could test a theory by seeing whether what it predicted took place. Such a decisive test sometimes could enable scientists to choose between two competing theories: the decisive observation could be regarded as neutral and therefore an unbiased way of choosing a theory.

This attractively simple account has been modified because of general recognition of the fact that observations cannot have an entirely neutral character, and also because of a stronger sense of the sinuousness of scientific theories. It is too simple to assume that scientific theories can have only two outcomes in relation to experimental data: either total success of a simple and straightforward kind, or failure of the kind that leads to dismissal. Theories can be modified, and an attractive theory that fits some data very well can be worth modifying if in one or two instances it is initially less successful.

It is true that there are referential constraints on the sciences. The constraints are facts; scientific theories must fit facts; and facts are in some sense items to which we refer. However, there are good reasons for saying, in P.F. Strawson's words, that a fact 'is not something in the world'. Facts are, as we have seen, themselves permeated by theory or theory-like elements. Furthermore, it is more appropriate to speak of facts as 'constraints' on the sciences than to use less guarded language: an unwelcome fact need not destroy a theory, but may merely force modification of it, and entirely successful prediction on the other hand does not ensure that a theory will be accepted for all time. Having said this, we should stress that there *are* referential constraints on scientific theories. No matter how beautiful and coherent a theory is, and even if the facts against which it is tested will be seen through a framework derived from the theory, the theory can still fail in relation to the facts. Scientific theories are in that sense not self-contained in the way in which fugues and paintings are.

Are there any constraints on an ethical theory? The answer must be 'Yes', although the constraints are less easy to classify than those on scientific theories. Consider, as an opening example, the Kantian ethical theory, with its assumption that moral decisions are always decisions of principle and with its apparatus of moral rules tested by the categorical imperative. It has been possible for someone to hold this theory, interpret moral decisions within the framework of the theory, and yet to become increasingly uncomfortable with the way in which the theory handled (or failed to handle) cases that did not straightforwardly seem to involve matters of principle or that were exceptional in one way or another. Such a person might well feel that there was something about life itself, to put it very broadly, that made the theory unacceptable. Having said this, one must add that of course many people still accept Kantian ethical theory as valid. But then we should recall Max Planck's famous comment, that 'a new scientific truth does not triumph by convincing its opponents and making them see the light, but rather because its opponents eventually die, and a new generation grows up that is familiar with it'. The process by which a theory loses or gains ground, whether in the sciences or in ethics, can be slow.

The general point to be made here is that people often discover something about moral conduct or about values that does not fit the ethical theories they started out with, and which cannot be regarded as 'programmed' by these theories or as, for that matter, straightforwardly derivable from other theory-like elements in their thinking about moral conduct or about values. Someone may, for example, enter on a way of life which she or he has learned from childhood to regard as highly desirable, and discover the values afforded by that life to be unsatisfactory. Someone who has believed that an exploitative practice, say slavery, is entirely justifiable may find, after a close and prolonged exposure to the practice, that she or he can no longer endorse it. No doubt in cases like these there are likely to be theoretical elements which dispose a person to recognise the unsatisfactoriness of what previously had been believed about moral conduct or about values: someone who holds a religious view that places a negative value on human degradation may be quicker to condemn slavery than someone who does not. But to say this is not to say that the changed position is simply a derivation from theory-like elements that make it possible: if it were, then presumably these theory-like elements would have ruled out the initial beliefs. Rather, we are confronted with an ethical analogue to a general truth about perception, that some things will be seen only by the prepared eye. And the general point remains: that in ethics as in the sciences a strongly held theory is not always confirmed by experience.

There are of course enormous differences within this similarity. It used to be thought that the wrongness of a scientific theory could be, as it were, 'read off' from the result of a crucial experiment. It is now more commonly believed that data contain within themselves interpretative elements, and that the use of data is itself a complex interpretative process. However, the interpretative element in what someone experiences during a close look at slavery, or in the experience of what a way of life has to offer, is even more pronounced. There is far more latitude in whether a practice is seen as abominable or a way of life as sterile. It is extremely natural, as a result, to say that so-and-so saw the practice *as* abominable, and saw the way of life *as* sterile. Coming to see slavery as abominable and a certain way of life as sterile may be more akin to coming to see a duck-rabbit as a duck than to seeing a duck for the first time. But the transformation cannot usually take place without prolonged experience of relevant sorts. It is important both to recognise how judgements of values and of morality can arise first-hand out of experience, and at the same time to recognise that it is even less plausible to view these judgements as 'read off' from the experience than it is to regard scientific judgements as 'read off' from the results of experiments.

With the qualifications and cautions just suggested, it does make sense to regard ethical theories as tested by and vulnerable to life experience. We must remember, though, that (as in the case of the sciences, but in a much more pronounced way) the experience against which an ethical theory is tested will be permeated with theoretical elements, borrowed from the theory itself or elsewhere. Thus in ethics, as in the sciences, the test of experience in some cases will be too easy for a theory, in that the experiences can incorporate a bias in favour of the theory. The bias also can run the other way, especially when a new theory is being considered. If an ethical theory runs counter to some of our 'intuitions' about what is right or what is just, there is room to reconsider the intuitions.

One further point should be made about ethical theory. It is very tempting to think of ethical thought as taking place on at most three levels: the level of particular judgements ('It would be wrong to take this money'), the level of general rules ('Stealing is wrong'), and the level of theory and abstraction ('One should act only on maxims that one could will to become universal laws', or 'Maximise the total happiness of sentient beings'). This may be a risky oversimplification.

In the sciences, theories or theory-like constructions occur at more than one level. The theory of relativity, for example, is at a higher and more abstract level than the theories that explain magnetism or the behaviour of winds. Utilitarianism, which in its simplest form holds that one should always maximise the happiness of sentient beings, is an example of a highly general and abstract theory in ethics. The scientific analogue should encourage us to leave room for the idea that highly general ethical theories, such as utilitarianism, are compatible with theories of moderate generality, concerned with such things as social institutions, human dignity, or aid to the unfortunate who cannot help themselves.

NOTES AND REFERENCES

Kant's view of the difficulty of knowing whether the maxim of an action rested solely on moral grounds is to be found in *Foundations of the Metaphysics of Morals*, p. 23 of the Beck translation. Thomas Nagel's 'Moral luck' is contained in his collection, *Mortal Questions* (Cambridge, 1979). Arthur Adkins's discussion of the assumptions about merit of Homeric Greece is to be found in his *Merit and Responsibility: A Study in Greek Values* (Chicago, 1975). Nietzsche's remark that someone of character will have a typical experience is to be found in *Beyond Good and Evil*, trans. W. Kaufmann (New York, 1960), p. 80.

Examples of the lines of thought that lead to denial of the 'neutral given' can be found in T.S. Kuhn's *The Structure of Scientific Revolutions*, 2nd edn. (Chicago, 1970) and in L. Foster and J. Swanson (eds), *Experience and Theory* (Amherst, Mass., 1970), especially the essays by Nelson Goodman and P.F. Strawson. For the notion of 'referential constraints' in the sciences, see T.S. Kuhn's remark in 'Reflections on my critics', in I. Lakatos and A. Musgrave (eds), *Criticism and the Growth of Knowledge* (Cambridge, 1970), that 'nature cannot be forced into an arbitrary set of conceptual boxes' (p. 263). See also I. Scheffler, *Science and Subjectivity* (New York, 1967). Strawson's claim that 'a fact is not something in the world' is to be found in his 'Truth', in G. Pitcher (ed.), *Truth* (Englewood Cliffs, N.J.: 1964), p. 37. Max Planck's comment about scientific progress is to be found in his *Scientific Autobiography and Other Papers*, trans. F. Gaynor (New York, 1949), and is quoted in Kuhn's *The Structure of Scientific Revolutions*, p. 151.

For a conception of ethical theory very different from mine, see John Rawls, *A Theory of Justice* (Cambridge, Mass., 1971), pp. 46–53. During the discussion of moral progress later in this book, the reader might ask herself or himself what kind of 'reflective equilibrium' an ethical theorist might have been able to arrive at two or three hundred years ago on the subject of women's proper role in society. Different questions of course arise if one wonders what Rawls's method yields on the issues of animal rights. What I am suggesting is that, despite the radical conclusions about distribution of wealth and power that Rawls draws, his conception of how ethical theories are generated and tested has a somewhat morally conservative bias, in that the possibilities for criticism of existing entrenched moral assumptions are limited.

Chapter 5

Difficult Cases and Moral Progress

We can return to the question of whether we need ethical theory at all. An ethical theory gives us a way of interpreting obligation, but perhaps the common understanding of obligation is good enough for practical and moral purposes. An ethical theory provides a decision procedure, at least for moral choices, that goes beyond or supplements familiar rules of conduct; a theory may also provide a way of assessing the moral worth of individuals. But perhaps familiar rules of conduct, and familiar ways of assessing moral worth, are adequate?

Let us label moral common sense (or common-sense morality) what all of us have without special aid from ethical theory. The argument of this chapter will be that moral common sense is inadequate in two regards. First, it needs help with difficult cases. Secondly, it risks moral complacency, in that it gives an insufficient standpoint from which to criticise the accepted practices of one's own culture and time. Both of these are reasons why we need ethical theory.

Difficult cases, as I define them, are cases that do not neatly fit the apparatus of familiar moral rules. This can occur for a number of reasons. Someone may have to choose between alternatives each of which involves the likelihood of some harm falling upon others, or some good being missed; but no familiar moral rule clearly applies, or two or more familiar rules seem to apply but point in opposite directions. Such is the case of a government official deciding whether budgetary cuts should come from health-care programmes or from aid to underdeveloped countries, or the case of Sartre's pupil, who must desert his dependent mother if he is to fight for the Free French. Alternatively someone may have to make a choice in a situation in which only one familiar moral rule applies, but there are circumstances about the case which might give one the sense that in this particular case what the rule enjoins is not the best choice. Perhaps some people will indirectly be led to suffer, or to fail to have their needs met, if the choice enjoined by the familiar rule is taken. The case of the man who can get the medicine needed by his dying wife only by stealing it is of this sort.

One way of dealing with such cases is simply to deny that they exist. Someone in whose view moral virtue is a matter of following the rules can in any case either fasten on to one familiar moral rule that applies to the case and follow it (ignoring any other rule that seems to point in an opposite direction), or, if no familiar moral rule seems to apply, can decide that the problem at hand is not a moral problem at all, but rather one of expediency. This last manoeuvre appears to be especially common among people who make decisions like the one of where the budget cuts should go. One of the sources of the idea that morality hardly enters into politics, the business of government, or the conduct of foreign policy is that simple traditional morality is so often useless in these areas.

A more sophisticated manoeuvre is to resort to casuistry, to invent new rules and modify old ones in order to make cases come out right. The lack of success of casuistry was discussed in Chapter 2. One further point should be made here. Insofar as casuists are not engaged in simple word play with moral formulas, but are genuinely trying to make cases come out right, then we need to account for their sense of what it is for a case to come out right. If we can get hold of something that accounts for a casuist's notion of which way a familiar moral rule should be modified to deal with a special case, and the casuist's notion of when the casuistical work has or has not been done well, then we will have something far more valuable than casuistry.

Casuistry builds on an element within moral common sense: the assumption that normally moral problems will be solved by an appeal to a suitable generalisation. But moral common sense has other elements in it, which enable most people to be suspicious of casuistry. We can tell when the word-play becomes contrived and the resultant formulas artificial. Where does this leave us with regard to difficult cases?

There is a sophisticated strain within moral common sense that tells us that, confronted with a difficult case, we are to look at the circumstances of the case and use our judgement. Looking at the circumstances involves *noticing* features that might be important, and generally being aware of what might be *salient*. Judgement here requires a sense of what is important, which in turn has to do not only with value judgements (judgements, for example, of which losses or gains on various people's parts to regard as major and which as trifling) but also with judgements of fact (judgements, for example, that something which now looks insignificant could have major consequences later, or that an event of a certain sort could change someone's life). All of this requires experience. Just as the experienced detective presumably notices things that simply do not catch the attention of the average person, so the experienced moral agent can be perceptive, and can also have a practised sense of what is salient, and also of what is likely to have major consequences. Something like this appears to be at work in the account presented in Aristotle's *Nicomachean Ethics* and in the account found in the Confucian *Doctrine of the Mean*. Both Aristotle's and the Confucian works on ethics are philosophically very sophisticated, but they are also close to elements of our moral common sense.

In this respect we are still on a pretheoretical level, exploring what moral common sense has to offer and looking also for clues as to what can be built on it. The strain of moral common sense just discussed is useful in pointing us towards experience and judgement in difficult cases, but one might hope for more help. At least one could be told what kinds of morally relevant features of a case to look for, or how to collate what one perceives. It is at this point that the need for theory becomes clearest. But, in formulating this need, we must be clear about how much we want from a theory, and about how much we might be willing to settle for. John McDowell has suggested that the desire to avoid 'vertigo' can lead to unwarranted assumptions about the character that an ethical theory must have. It is perhaps possible to expect too much from ethical theory.

Let us distinguish between a strong set of expectations for ethical theory and a weak set of expectations. This distinction is especially important for my argument, because in the chapters that follow I shall offer something that might satisfy a weak set of expectations but not a strong set. It is as important to see what will not be offered as it is to see what will be offered.

A strong set of expectations would be for an ethical theory that can accomplish the following in relation to difficult cases.

1 Provide criteria for which features of a case are morally relevant and which are not (that is, tell one what to look for).
2 Provide precise criteria for how the relevant features of a case are to be weighed once they have been identified, so that one has a precisely formulable decision procedure.
3 Do the foregoing in such a way that no special intelligence or sensitivity is required to apply the theory: that is, persons of moderate intelligence who accept the theory can apply it and expect in the general run of cases to get roughly the same results.

Kant's ethical theory certainly seems as if it is designed to meet all of the above expectations, as does classical utilitarianism. Kant's remarks about judgement in *Foundations of the Metaphysics of Morals*, along with the whole of the *Metaphysical Principles of Virtue*, might, however, make one hesitate in that assessment. It is true both of Kant's theory and of utilitarianism that they seem far more likely in the abstract to satisfy the strong set of expectations than they seem when one begins to apply them to difficult cases.

A weak set of expectations is for a theory that accomplishes the following.

1 Provides criteria for which features of a case are morally relevant and which are not (that is, tells one what to look for).
2 Provides rough criteria for how relevant features of a case are to be weighed once they have been identified, so that one has a rough sense of degrees of importance.

In practice, no ethical theory yet devised has been able, when applied, to meet the strong set of expectations, although some theories seem designed with the hope that they will. There are a number of obstacles to this hope, but one is especially serious. This is the problem of objective description. It is not always immediately obvious whether something should be classified as pleasure or as painful, whether someone is happy, whether someone has got what she preferred or not, or whether a given action could be classified as stealing or as breaking a promise. One can provide criteria, but these will have to be supplemented by judgement, and there will be room for disagreement and argument. These are all points that Kant (I think reluctantly) recognised. They seriously compromise the third expectation in the strong set: that persons of moderate intelligence can expect in general to get roughly the same results from the theory. In practice it has become increasingly clear, since Kant's time, that people who accept his theory can apply it in very different ways and obtain very different results. There is room for a similar judgement about utilitarianism, even apart from difficulities in and disagreements about prediction.

The sciences to a considerable degree get around the problem of objective description by substituting judgements of quantity for most (but obviously not for all) judgements of quality. Systems and instruments of measurement provide objectivity of description, at least within the framework of a given theory, that the subjects (history and the social sciences) that describe and explain human behaviour for the most part do not attain. I have argued elsewhere that history and the social sciences (with the possible exception of economics) cannot attain this kind of objectivity. There are standards by which some descriptions can be faulted as biased and not objective; and some accounts can be shown to be more objective than others; but this does not mean that there is an ideally objective description of a historical event or a social process which is the last word in the same way that 'The temperature in the pasture is twenty degrees centigrade' is the last word on the temperature in the pasture. The actions of rational creatures, such as history and the social sciences describe and explain, are of course the domain of ethics; and, if there is no ideally objective description of them, there are thereby limits to the objectivity we can expect from ethics. This does not mean, of course, in history, the social sciences, or in ethics, that 'anything goes', or that all accounts are of equal value; but it does mean that there is always room for redescription and for argument.

Thus there is reason to believe that a major obstacle to an ethical theory's meeting the strong set of expectations is permanent. Perhaps then we should lower our expectations to the level of the weak set? This would involve learning to live with lack of precision, and with the prospect of reasonable people differing both in some of their descriptions of human actions and in their judgements of these actions.

An ethical theory that met the weak set of expectations would be better than nothing: that is to say, moral common sense supplemented by such a theory would be better than unsupplemented moral common sense. After all, we do need any help that might be available with the difficult cases. Aristotle and the Confucians speak quite helpfully of experience and judgement in relation to these cases. But it would be helpful also to know just what is made possible by experience, and in relation to what considerations judgement is to be exercised. Any further organising principles, telling us what to look for, and how seriously to weigh it once we have found it, would be to the good.

Difficult cases thus provide a rationale for looking for ethical theory, even theory that satisfies only the weak set of expectations. But easy cases also provide a rationale. When Confucius said 'Your honest countryman is the spoiler of morals', he may have been thinking of the dangers of someone's following traditional moral rules even in difficult cases in which countervailing factors should be taken seriously. But he may have been thinking also of the possibility that some traditional moral rules are inadequate. If so, the moral order that they endorse, and the social order that they underwrite, can be improved upon; and the honest countryman who has accepted the traditional rules at face value is likely to be the greatest enemy of this improvement.

This is something that we are very aware of in relation to practices in the past such as slavery and the subjection of women. It is hard to shake one's wonder that decent people, people who in most of the transactions of everyday life appear to have been reasonably kind and responsible, supported such practices, and that not only honest countrymen but also philosophers like Aristotle were so mistaken. This should encourage us to be less complacent about our own moral and social order.

Before we discuss some contemporary challenges to this moral and social order, something should be said on the general topic of moral progress. By moral progress I mean neither progress in ethical theory nor progress in the way people actually behave, but rather progress in degree of acceptability of the moral requirements that are widely recognised in a society. The moral requirements that are widely recognised in our society are superior to (more acceptable than) those in earlier societies, at least in such matters as treatment of women, treatment of strangers and the very poor, treatment of debtors, etc. – one can say this without holding that present arrangements are ideal – and in this sense there has been some moral progress. In this sense also there may well be room for further moral progress.

One fairly obvious but important point is that a great deal of what most of us would agree to have been moral progress has come about through the enlargement of sympathies. That is, one of the factors promoting better attitudes toward slavery, the subjection of women, the imprisonment of debtors, etc., has been increased willingness to extend to victims of these practices the degree of sympathy that one extends to people of one's own sex, race, and social class. Many people would argue, indeed, that such a broadening of sympathy is the key to a wide range of moral problems.

One such person was Mencius, a Confucian philosopher of the fourth century BC. There is a story in Mencius's works which neatly illustrates the point. A king had balked at having a sacrificial ox killed, and instead had ordered it removed and a lamb to be slaughtered instead. People muttered that this was to save expense, but Mencius later asks the king whether it was not rather that he had looked at the frightened ox and could not bear to cause its death. The king admits that this was so. There is obvious irony in causing the death of an animal one does not see while sparing the animal one does see, but Mencius points out also that saving the ox is evidence of sympathy in the king's nature. If the king has failed to cherish his people it comes from not exerting his sympathy. The king has been spending heavily on military preparations, because of his territorial ambitions, thus over-burdening the economy. 'Nowadays, the means laid down for the people are sufficient neither for the care of parents nor for the support of wife and children. In good years life is always hard, while in bad years there is no way of escaping death.'

Mencius urges the king to 'go back to fundamentals'. What is most fundamental is that sympathy which Mencius (like David Hume two thousand years later) argued to be inherent in human nature. The implication is that if one can strip away the layers of distraction and of selfish concern, and can look clearly at the people affected by one's actions, one is far more likely to behave morally. There seems to be much truth to this, in that by and large immoral actions hurt others, and people who commit immoral actions by and large are insensitive both to the feelings and to details of the consequent lives of their victims. There seems to be some truth also to the view that extending sympathy, to those far away as well as those close at hand, and to those unlike oneself as well as to those who are very similar, is a powerful engine of moral progress.

It will not do however to overstate the case. Someone can be very sensitive to, and sympathetic with, the feelings of everyone affected by her or his actions, and still make the wrong choices. In the case of Gauguin, or Sartre's pupil, or the person responsible for deciding whether to cut the budget for health care or for aid to underdeveloped countries, it is very hard to argue that the exercise of sympathy by itself will get the right answer. (Nor would Mencius have made such a strong claim.) Neither is it plausible to say that what most of us would agree is moral progress is always, simply and straightforwardly, just a matter of the extension of sympathy.

One example must suffice. This is the moral progress in America represented ultimately by the decision, in the mid-nineteenth century, that slavery was morally unacceptable, and represented concretely by the abolition of slavery. As a case this has a number of features that reveal something about the development of moral common sense, and it is worth describing these before proceeding to the question of whether the progress was just a matter of the extension of sympathy.

First, the moral progress in America in relation to slavery must be placed in a larger context. It is a moment in a larger change. Since the eighteenth century a shift has been taking place in Western moral common sense, from a morality that enjoined protection of the physical well-being of all, and respect for the dignity of a few, to a morality that not only enjoins protection of the physical well-being of all but also accords dignity to all. As practical expressions of this change one may note the abolition of slavery, the Reform Act of 1867 in England, women's suffrage, and the Equal Rights Amendment in America (whose vicissitudes indicate that the change is not complete). The leading theoretician of this moral revolution was undoubtedly Immanuel Kant; to say this does not imply a strong direct influence on Kant's part, but merely that his philosophy gives a clear, powerful, and early theoretical expression of the principles at work.

The moral change just outlined does not involve complete repudiation of what came before. The extension of dignity to all humans after all has roots in Christianity, whose ideas predate the beginning of the change by a very long time. However, it would be simple-minded to insist that those who upheld the values of a rigidly hierarchical society were in some sense unfaithful to, or in contradiction with, Christianity. They had their interpretation of the basic ideas, in which dignity was restricted to the realm of religious salvation, which is after all what is discussed in the New Testament. We of the twentieth century have widened our interpretation. The two opposing moral views could both be considered Christian.

Thus moral change, at least in this case, is not sheer reversal. It is not the case that something had been thought but now the entire opposite is thought. The new consensus (which in our case is still developing) incorporates elements of the old: what is now believed, but had not been believed, is based at least in part on moral assumptions which were shared by both sides of the debate, although perhaps interpreted in different ways.

This becomes clearer if we look at the particular case of the abolition of slavery in America. It is not true that those who defended slavery before the Civil War placed no value on the welfare of black people or that all those who rejected slavery placed significant value on the welfare of blacks. Eugene Genovese paraphrases the position of George Fitzhugh, one of the leading defenders of slavery, as follows: 'Slavery, with its principle of responsibility of one man for another, led to less hardship and despair than capitalism, with its principle of every man for himself, for at least the worker had a community to appeal to other than one based on a cash nexus.' The slave thus, in Fitzhugh's view, was better off than a worker in the capitalist industry of the North, who not only had to work long hours in poor conditions, but also had no social protection if he became ill or disabled. Fitzhugh is attractive to Marxist historians like Genovese in part because, in his hands, the defence of slavery becomes an attack on capitalism. Nor is Fitzhugh unique. J.H. Hammond argued that the control of some people over others is inevitable in any society. The Northern factory owner owns his workers as surely as the Southern plantation owner owns his; the difference is in the degree of beneficence, and of responsibility to the workers.

A great deal of the argument against slavery rested on appeals to the intrinsic value of freedom and human dignity. But these appeals should not be taken as necessarily expressing a full-blown extension of sympathy to the slaves, or as advocating anything like equal rights. To assume this is to make a mistake like that John Stuart Mill imputed to Bentham, of confounding all disinterested feelings with the desire for the general happiness. Some people who favoured the abolition of slavery also opposed anything like racial integration, and there was not enough concern about what happened to former slaves after they were freed. The widespread extension of sympathy to the descendants of former slaves had to wait another hundred years. To the extent that the abolition of slavery represented a shift in moral common sense, it was not so much a result of extension of sympathy as it was a victory for principles concerned with human dignity, and these principles were not generally given as strong an interpretation as we would believe they deserved.

Two points should be made about what this case illustrates. One is that insofar as proponents of various ethical theories, including utilitarianism, would agree that moral progress did take place, this suggests that *any* ethical theory might well make room, at some level, for principles having to do with human dignity. This can be accomplished in more than one way; but one obvious way is for a theory whose fundamental claim is that X is what is ethically important to insist that human dignity, generally speaking, is an instance of, or is conducive to, X, and that therefore secondary principles concerned with human dignity should be taken seriously. John Stuart Mill's *On Liberty* is an example of this construction of a secondary level of theory in relation to liberty, and no doubt a similar utilitarian treatment of human dignity is possible.

A second point is that it would be naive to assume, just because a major moral change has taken place in attitudes towards human dignity, that it is the only major moral change that has taken place during the last two hundred years, or that the next moral change that is needed or will take place also concerns attitudes towards human dignity. There certainly have been changes (noted earlier) in prevalent moral attitudes towards privilege, and towards extreme economic and social inequality; and *this* shift in moral common sense owes a great deal to Jeremy Bentham's insistence that (in the matter of happiness) each person should count for one, plus obvious facts about the marginal contribution to happiness of increments of money and goods. The next shifts in moral common sense are more likely to be continuations of this than of the change in attitudes toward human dignity, which seems nearly complete.

Three possible shifts in moral common sense deserve mention. At the risk of disappointing the reader I should say that I have no confidence that any of the three, singly, is highly likely; although the likelihood that at least one of the three will take place seems very great. First of all, it may very well be that, over the next few hundred years, there will be a further shift in moral attitudes towards social and economic inequality within a society, so that degrees of inequality that seem to us tolerable will have come to seem morally unacceptable. Secondly, there may well come to be more widespread repugnance towards inequalities between members of one society and members of another. This could be manifested in an increased sense of responsibility for the poor in other societies. One of the things that hampers the work of organisations such as Oxfam is that current moral common sense regards anything that we do for the poor of other countries as supererogatory. This might not be the case in a few hundred years. Thirdly, there might come to be a widespread increased concern for the rights, or at least the welfare, of animals, along the lines advocated by such writers as Peter Singer.

For the purposes of our argument, what matters is not so much speculation about the future of moral common sense as the fact that options are open, and that we cannot be complacent about our present point of view. We cannot assume that what seems obviously morally acceptable is indeed morally acceptable. If we make such an assumption, we risk being in the position of those who endorsed slavery or of those who saw nothing wrong with the imprisonment of debtors or with the torture of those accused of crimes. The future of moral common sense may consist of a decline rather than progress, or there may be no significant change at all; but this does not alter the point that we cannot assume that everything endorsed by present-day moral common sense is thereby morally acceptable. We need a standpoint outside moral common sense from which to evaluate what at first seems morally obvious.

One must not overstate the case here. Within moral common sense there are many different elements, pointing in different directions; and furthermore these can be variously interpreted. The case of slavery suggests the strong possibility that any change in moral common sense will build on elements already present in it, and will in part be based on these. (For that matter ethical theories must to some degree appeal to elements already present in moral common sense.) Thus it would be wrong to deny that elements are already present in moral common sense that provide the basis for a criticism of it. My claim is that it is generally not very easy to formulate these elements, and that the process of criticism is facilitated if we do more than simply excavate what is contained in moral common sense.

Ethical theory can have the function of providing a clear standpoint from which to criticise moral common sense. Historically both Kant's theory and utilitarianism have played this role. They have both made it possible for people to view the moral assumptions of their culture with a kind of objectivity which the more simple-minded cultural relativists cannot grasp as possible, and to provide a reasoned basis for condemning practices that are generally considered morally acceptable. There is no reason to suppose that ethical theory cannot continue to play that role. If we wish to take a cool and independent look at what moral common sense treats as obvious, then ethical theory can be very helpful.

NOTES AND REFERENCES

John McDowell's discussion of 'vertigo' is to be found in his 'The concept of a person in ethical theory' (*Monist*, 1979). See especially footnote 38. My argument that the objectivity of history and the social sciences is necessarily limited is contained in 'Precision in history' (*Mind*, 1975). Confucius said 'Your honest countryman is the spoiler of morals' in the *Analects*, Book XVII, Chapter XIII, trans. W.E. Soothill (London, 1955), p. 193. The passage from Mencius is from *Mencius*, trans. D.C. Lau (Harmondsworth, 1970), Book I, Part A, 7, pp. 54–9.

An interesting discussion of progress in ethics is to be found in J.J.C. Smart, 'Ethics and science', University of Tasmania Occasional Paper 30 (1981). Genovese's discussion of the pro-slavery case is to be found in *The World the Slaveholders Made* (New York, 1971). The paraphrase of Fitzhugh is on p. 160. For useful background on the controversy see W.H. and J.H. Pease (eds), *The Anti-Slavery Argument* (New York, 1965), Gerald Sorin, *Abolitionism* (New York, 1972), and John L. Thomas, 'Romantic reform in America, 1815-1865', in David Brion Davis (ed.), *Ante-Bellum Reform* (New York, 1967).

Mill's comment on the variety of disinterested feelings is to be found in his 'Bentham', contained in *Utilitarianism and Other Writings*, ed. Mary Warnock (New York, 1962), p. 102. For Peter Singer's views on the treatment of animals, see *Animal Liberation* (New York, 1975), and also *Practical Ethics* (Cambridge, 1979).

Chapter 6

Utilitarianism and Value

The two major ethical theories that have already been useful in providing a basis for going beyond, and also for criticising, moral common sense are Kant's and utilitarianism. Each of these is capable of further development and modification. Alan Donagan's interesting *A Theory of Morality* in some ways represents an updating of Kantian theory. Utilitarianism now includes many different schools, and some of the utilitarian tradition is also carried on by philosophers who in Part Three will be classified and discussed as consequentialists.

At various points thus far I have provided arguments for thinking that Kantian theory, in any form that resembles the original, is seriously inadequate. The major inadequacy is that any theory like Kant's must claim that moral problems generally can be solved by means of a system of rules. Since Kant's time it has become increasingly obvious that no system of rules will be adequate to the task, and that the artificial elaborations of casuistry are not a credible supplement to general rules. The Kantian emphasis on respecting human dignity is of considerable value, but there is no reason why other theories, including utilitarianism, cannot incorporate a comparable emphasis; and, furthermore, we have pointed out that many ethical problems cannot be solved simply by giving paramount importance to respect for human dignity. There are a large number of problems like Gauguin's or the problem of the person who has to decide whether to cut the budget for health care or for aid to under-developed countries, and we need more help with these problems than Kantian theories can supply.

Utilitarianism does seem useful in relation to such problems. But utilitarianism has difficulties of its own. These are in one respect very different from the difficulties of Kantian theory. It is arguable that Kant's ethical theory, at least if one does not interpret Kant as being a 'rigorist', does not offer clearly wrong answers to any moral questions. The great fault is that, for a large number of questions, the theory offers no clear answers whatsoever, or rather the answers are left open until one resorts to the contrivances of casuistry or to special interpretations of the maxims and principles that may be involved. One may disagree with, say, Alan Donagan's views concerning abortion, but can arrive at a different view by a different interpretation of Kantian theory. The implications of utilitarianism, also, are not entirely clear in relation to some particular cases; but in addition utilitarianism has been charged with yielding results in some cases that are clearly wrong. One might draw the contrast here by saying that Kantian ethics at its worst can be accused of a well-meaning vagueness, and that utilitarianism at its worst can be accused of being counter-intuitive. One can say this without foreclosing either the possibility that some theory in the utilitarian tradition will not be vulnerable to the accusation of being counter-intuitive or the possibility that finally the best available theory will indeed turn out to be somewhat counter-intuitive.

In this chapter we shall examine utilitarianism in general, and in particular the accounts of value that are incorporated in utilitarian theories. My working assumptions will be, first, that 'utilitarianism' now denotes a cluster of theories rather than a single theory, and secondly that utilitarian theories come neatly apart into components. Thus it is useful to bear in mind the possibility of modifying utilitarian theories, and of recombining or abstracting elements.

Utilitarian theories have two major components. The theories concern, first and foremost, what should be done: they guide choices among alternative courses of action. This is based on a generalisation about value: that what is valuable is pleasure and the absence of pain, or happiness and the absence of suffering, or the satisfaction of human preferences, or the satisfaction of preferences generally. Something – call it X – is declared to be valuable, and the utilitarian conjoins this value generalisation to another, which links judgements of what we should do to judgements of consequences. Either we should do what has the best consequences (what will maximise X) or we should follow a moral rule or a policy general recognition of or adherence to which would have the best consequences (would maximise X), or we should act on motives or on the basis of attitudes which tend to produce the best consequences (tend to maximise X). This second component is what has been called consequentialism. Utilitarian theories are the conjunction of value generalisations of a certain sort with consequentialism.

We can take the value component of utilitarian theories apart further by asking the following questions.

1   Is what is valuable only psychological states?
2   Is the total of value at a given time the sum of values of psychological states?
3   Is it the case that all satisfactions (or satisfactions of some specific kind) and only these satisfactions are of value?

Utilitarians characteristically answer 'Yes' to all three questions. I shall argue that the answer to (1) is 'Yes', but that there is reason for doubting an answer of 'Yes' to (2) and strong reasons for answering

'No' to (3). This will amount to a rejection of the characteristic utilitarian position on value.

Some general remarks on our subject matter, and on the investigation we can bring to bear on it, are in order. Value theory has been in recent years the most neglected area of ethics. It has been neglected for a clear reason: the progress that one can make in it by analysis of our concepts or of common-sense assumptions is limited. Finally one has to make value judgements on the basis of the grounds that are available. In what follows, I shall argue that grounds are available, and that people are sometimes in a very good position to be confident of judgements of value. But it would be foolish to expect that one could arrive at value judgements that would satisfy everyone, or whose grounds would satisfy everyone.

Because of this, it is very tempting for an ethical theorist to finesse the problems of value theory, in effect refusing (with some qualifications) to make value judgements by treating all things within a certain category as equal. An excellent recent example of this is to be found in Richard Brandt's *A Theory of the Good and the Right*. Brandt maintains that all desires and aversions (on anyone's part) which are such that they would survive cognitive psychotherapy should be given weight proportionate to that with which they are had. Brandt terms cognitive psychotherapy, which is a process of confronting desires with relevant information in an 'ideally vivid way', a 'value-free reflection'. I have commented elsewhere on Brandt's view. It is enough for our present purposes to note that it is question-begging. Cognitive psychotherapy does not cure philistinism, and thus Brandt has begged the questions asked by Aristotle in Book I of the *Nicomachean Ethics*, by G.E. Moore in the final chapter of *Principia Ethica*, and by John Stuart Mill in his well-known discussion of the 'higher' and 'lower' pleasures. It may be that none of the arguments provided by Aristotle, Moore, or Mill, and for that matter none of the arguments of this chapter, can meet the highest standards of rigour, but the alternative of simply as much as possible avoiding value judgements is even less satisfactory.

With these limitations on what we can accomplish in mind, we can turn to the three questions about value which utilitarians characteristically answer positively.

1 G.E. Moore, who deviated from standard utilitarian positions in a number of ways, argued that the correct answer to the first question is 'No'. In a famous thought experiment he invited his readers to intuit the intrinsic value of a beautiful world which has not been and never will be experienced by anyone and that of an exceedingly ugly world which has not been and will not be experienced by anyone. Moore claimed that the beautiful world in itself is better than the ugly, and hence that there is some value apart from psychological states.

Consideration of Moore's claim brings us closer to a question that we must begin to answer: what counts as evidence or good reason for a claim of value? Moore's appeal to 'intuition' amounts to a non-answer, in that all he meant by calling certain judgements intuitions was that they could not be demonstrated, and hence if true were self-evident. Judgements of what is obligatory were, in his view, intuitive only in a 'psychological sense', in that they could be confirmed or refuted by an investigation of consequences.

'Intuitions' that something is valuable must, in this account, be an extremely heterogeneous lot. The most uninformed judgements, influenced by prejudice, would count as 'intuitions' as surely as would relatively unbiased judgements made as a result of intimate acquaintance with what is judged. Furthermore, there is a strong case for saying that there are some judgements of value that we simply are not in a position to make. If someone asks me 'Were the typical daily experiences of a medieval Japanese samurai of high or low value?', or 'If there is such a thing as the Buddhist nirvana is it worth attaining?', I am at a loss. Only if I have experienced something very like that the value of which is in question, or if I can imaginatively put myself in such a state with good assurance that no crucial element is being left out, am I in a good position to make an independent judgement. One can of course rely on the reports or on the inferred judgements of others. One might say, for example, 'People who actually lived as Japanese samurai appeared on the whole to be satisfied with their lives, and they had their wits about them', or 'People who purportedly have been close to the Buddhist nirvana, and who talked about their experiences, praised them highly'. Reports or inferred judgements need not, of course, automatically be accepted. If drug-takers or idiots praise their experiences it may be just that their standards are disastrously low; indeed, one of the effects of certain drugs might be drastic lowering of standards. As Aristotle pointed out in his investigation of value, in considering people's opinions about what is most valuable one must always consider the source of judgements. We are most likely to trust the judgements of value made by people who have had a variety of experiences, and thus are able to make comparisons, and who have an unimpaired ability to continue to have a variety of experiences along with what we would consider an unclouded mind in judging them.

What basis do we have for a judgement of the value of an unexperienced (and never to be experienced) beautiful or ugly world? In putting the question in this way, I wish to suggest the extreme oddity of Moore's thought experiment. It is a little like saying to someone, 'After reading twenty books and viewing some of the art of the period you finally have some slight sense of what it would have been like to have been a Japanese samurai; now try deciding what it would be like to be a beautiful unexperienced world.' Our sense of value, after all, is based either on personal experience, imaginative reconstruction, or the reports or inferred judgements of others; and all of the other 'intuitions' of value reported by Moore were presumably derived from these sources. In this perspective Moore's thought experiment begins to look exceedingly bizarre, and the question it is designed to answer loses the appearance of having a clear meaning.

This suggests two possible responses to the question 'Is what is valuable only psychological states?' One is that the question is flatly meaningless; the other is that there is no basis for an answer other than 'Yes'. Any choice between these can be finally justified only by a book-length discussion of theories of meaning; instead I shall supply merely some brief remarks as partial justifications for my choice of the second response. This partial justification is based on the fact that judgements of value are connected to more than just those factors in experience that provide a basis for them. They also are connected to preferences, and to decisions of what should be pursued. Moore's judgement of the value of the beautiful unexperienced world may have been disconnected from any basis in experience, apart from one's general tendency to respond favourably to what is labelled 'beautiful' and negatively to what is labelled 'ugly'. But clearly it is connected to all sorts of choices in the real world concerning such things as the management of parks and scenic attractions. For this reason it seems to me that the question 'Is what is valuable only psychological states?' is meaningful even if there is no basis for any answer other than 'Yes', and even if for that matter it is very difficult to imagine what such a basis could be.

Now it may be felt that I have thus far ignored the most serious objection to the claim that what is valuable is only psychological states. Someone who holds something like a Kantian view of morality may believe that to assign all value to psychological states is to beg the question in favour of the consequentialism that will be argued for in Part Three of this book. That something morally right is done, it may be urged, in itself has very great value; that something wicked is done has in itself great negative value. These values must be reckoned with, quite apart from the values or disvalues of the psychological states of moral agents or of those affected by their actions.

As a preliminary point, it should be noted that Kant himself never made such a claim. Kant's remarks about value were, to be sure, very rudimentary. But he did affirm the great positive value of a 'good will'; and it is open to a consequentialist to agree with Kant on this point, and to urge that the value of the will of a moral agent is one of the most important features (or perhaps even the most important feature) to be assessed in evaluating the action that expresses it. The 'consequences' of an action include everything that is the case if the action is performed and not otherwise, and in this sense the good will of an agent is included (assuming that the good will cannot be said to exist unless the action is performed). It is also open to a consequentialist to claim that morally right and morally wrong actions, apart from their obvious effects, characteristically create a 'moral climate', which is reflected in subtle but important ways in the psychology of everyone who is affected by them or who knows of them. This too is consistent with the claim that what is valuable is only psychological states.

If we subtract the value (or negative value) of the good or bad will of the moral agent, and the values inherent in the moral climate created by the agent's choice, what value is left to be assigned to the fact that something morally right or morally wrong has been done? How may we know about this free-floating value?

When the question is put in this last way, the answer, I think, is evident. We are left with our own very strong preference that morally right choices be made and that immoral actions not be performed, and this can be accounted for very well without postulating a mysterious free-floating value as its object. The value that adheres to the fact that a morally right or wrong action has been performed, apart from the psychological states of those involved, looks very much like an *ad hoc* theoretical construct, like, say, the aether that at one point was thought to surround the earth in order to save a physical theory. We prefer that immoral acts not be performed because of the suffering and other bad consequences that they typically lead to, and perhaps also because of the divided and unwholesome state of mind that they express, which may spread as a contagion to others. We may know from experience what it is to be a victim of someone else's immorality, or what it is to do something immoral (or to be on the verge of doing something immoral) oneself; or perhaps we can imaginatively reconstruct these experiences. What more need be said? Nothing in our experience gives us any basis for assigning independent value, positive or negative, to the fact that a morally right or wrong act has been performed.

2 The question of whether the total of value at a given time is the sum of values of psychological states is a very general and abstruse one. It may not seem at first clear why what we decide should matter. We should begin by pointing out that a great deal might hang on the answer to this question.

The answer first of all will determine, not just a subclause of the theory we finally can accept, but rather its entire character and what it can claim to accomplish. It would be very difficult for any theory that did not include an answer of 'Yes' to this question to meet the strong set of expectations discussed in Chapter 4. The early utilitarians projected the development of an ethics that would be scientific, in which disagreements could be resolved objectively by means of precise techniques. Crucial to this hope is the expectation that something that is good in a situation can be added to whatever else is good in the situation, with whatever is bad subtracted, to yield the total of the net goodness. Addition and subtraction are very models of objectivity and precision. The hope for this kind of objectivity, and for precision, is perhaps not irrevocably doomed if we decide that the total of value at a given time is not necessarily the sum of the values of psychological states. But, if we adopt this view, it may be difficult to determine what else should be weighed and just how it should be weighed; and the objectivity and precision looked for by the early utilitarians are to say the least in jeopardy.

Secondly, many would hold that the answer will determine what kind of society we would favour. There has been an especially lively controversy in recent years concerning the distribution of goods. Many philosophers have charged that utilitarians, by claiming that all that matters is the net total of whatever is good minus whatever is bad, have been indifferent to questions concerning who enjoys the goods and suffers the evils. In theory two societies could yield the same net total of goods minus what is bad even though in one almost all of the goods are enjoyed by a small minority and almost all of the evils are suffered by others whereas in the other the goods and evils are more equally shared. It is held that we intuitively judge the second society to be more just, and hence to be preferable, but that there is no room for this judgement within utilitarianism.

To this utilitarians frequently reply that it is a fact that whatever people want (money, power, social status, etc.) very generally has diminishing marginal utility, however utility is measured. One hundred dollars will provide a far smaller increment of happiness, or of whatever else is good, to a rich person than to a poor one. This being so, utilitarians will tend to favour equal distributions of whatever people want, except in instances in which benefits for those already well off are so considerable as to yield more value than might be lost by those who are not well off: a utilitarian might favour a policy that yielded millions of additional dollars for those who were wealthy at the cost of a very slight financial loss for those who were less well off. But in the nature of things such policies are rarely if ever available: the typical choice is between a policy that yields slight additional value for those who are already well off and a policy that yields considerable additional value for those who are not well off, or between a policy that asks for slight sacrifices from those who are well off and a policy that asks for considerable sacrifices from those who are not well off. Thus it is not clear whether in practice there is much difference if any between utilitarians and their opponents on this issue. What difference there is may be more one of theoretical models.

In any case, how are we to decide the issue? Ethical philosophy has come full circle (or, some might say, has retreated) since the publication of Moore's *Principia Ethica*, and once again there are many who would resolve the issue by means of intuition. The intuition asked for is once again rather like what Moore asked for in the case of the beautiful and ugly unexperienced worlds: it is a contemplative one. One inspects models of societies which provide equal and unequal distributions of what people want (actual societies do not serve the purpose, both because no one is confident about how the sums should go and also because it turns out to be impossible to find actual cases about which utilitarians and their opponents on this issue disagree). One is then asked to intuit the following: that of two societies in which the total of goodness is the same, the one with the more equal distribution of goodness is better. The invitation, as in the case of the beautiful and ugly unexperienced worlds, is really to say how one *feels* about the two alternatives. One normally responds favourably to what is beautiful and negatively to what is ugly; and in the same way one normally responds favourably to a highly equal distribution of what is good, and negatively to a highly unequal distribution. In both cases a utilitarian can explain why we normally have these responses, and why it makes sense to have them. What is beautiful, after all, normally has a role in increasing the total of human satisfactions, as does more equal distribution of what people want.

Now it may seem that the only position consistent with what I have been saying is that there is in fact no basis for judging whether or not the total of value at a given time is the sum of values of psychological states. After all, any attempt to sense what it would be like to be an egalitarian or an inegalitarian society would be only slightly less absurd than an attempt to sense what it would be like to be a beautiful or an ugly unexperienced world. Nevertheless, I think that there is reason to support the view that the total of value at a given time is not necessarily the sum of the values of psychological states. The reason seems to me not to be at all strong, and merely to provide a ground for doubt of the utilitarian position on this matter. But it is better to mention it than to say nothing at all. What follows is both speculative and sketchy.

First, we must say more about the conditions under which someone is in a position to be confident of an ethical judgement. A paradigm case is one in which a person of some wisdom and maturity has had prolonged experience of a way of life or of a set of experiences, and judges its value. A strong response to the question 'How do you know that X is of high (or low) value?' is 'Over a period of time I have tried X'; although, as I have already indicated, in weighing the response we take into account our estimate of the person making it. Experience can put us in a good position to be confident of judgements of value. Under certain circumstances, imaginative reconstruction of a way of life or of a set of experiences can also put us in such a position: sometimes we can say, 'Even though I have not tried it, I know what it is like.'

Sometimes contact with others who have had the relevant experiences also has weight, especially if one can claim some sense of what their experiences are like. One can say, 'I have seen people who have tried X, and what their lives were like.' The authority of those who have experienced something, or who have achieved some imaginative reconstruction of it, can also have some weight, as can reasoning based on similarity between what is being judged and what one already knows the value of.

It would be wrong to assume that the only ethical judgements for which experience can give warrant are judgements of value. Directly or indirectly, experience can put us in a position to be confident of judgements concerning what ought to be done or what is morally wrong. The role of indirect experience is obvious: if we know that people to whom X is done generally are thoroughly miserable thereafter, this normally (unless there are special considerations, or X is justified punishment) puts us in a good position to be confident of a judgement that X is morally wrong. In some cases, reading about the effects of X may be about as good as actually seeing them. There are other cases, though, in which realities count for more than descriptions. Someone may think that a practice sounds innocuous and, after witnessing the practice and its effects, decide otherwise. It makes sense to say that someone is in an especially good position to judge the moral acceptability of X who has witnessed X and its effects over a period of time. Here again, in giving weight to such a judgement we take into account our estimate of the character of the person who makes it.

Are we ever in a position to make a judgement of a whole such that we can say that the value of the whole is not simply the sum of the values of the parts? My answer is 'Yes': what we can experience or get an imaginative sense of is not limited to psychological states of an individual at a moment. It might be tempting to suppose that what we can experience or imaginatively grasp always is limited to 'I (or some other person) here and now'. But in fact our possibilities extend beyond this, in two directions: we can have a sense of the experience of a person for a period of time (perhaps a life), and we can have a sense of the experience, mood, or moral climate found in a group of people (perhaps a society). Both of these points, if correct, are important to ethics.

With regard to the first, it should be pointed out that we frequently have a sense of a person's life (such as our own) as having an integrity and a structure of meanings of its own, so that we interpret certain episodes in terms of purposes fulfilled, thwarted, or abandoned, and other episodes as apprenticeship, postponement, deviation, or fruition. When people who are not philosophers talk about the 'meaning of life', or worry about whether a certain kind of life may be lacking in 'meaning', the focus is not on the sum of satisfactions or of anything else. Rather, there is a sense that a life should have a structure in which certain things make sense in the light of certain other things. The meaning of life is not entirely unlike the meaning of a play.

Because of this, it seems very implausible to regard the total values to be found in a life as merely the sum of the values in particular moments. People towards the end of their lives sometimes find, or fail to find, a summary value that has a good deal to do with significance and with interrelatedness of episodes. (One thinks of Wittgenstein on his deathbed.) It would be ignoring this to regard the value of life as just a sum.

It is more difficult to speak of the other way in which the possibilities of our imaginative experience extend beyond the 'I (or another person) here and now'. There certainly is no warrant for speaking of anything like a group mind. But it is a fact that we do experience individuals, including ourselves, in ways which are permeated with social meanings. Such matters as social class, role in a family structure, economic function, antecedents and aspirations are all very much features of individuals with whom we are acquainted. Group-related qualities are part of what constitutes an individual in society: just as a moment's consciousness contains meanings and significance which point backwards and forwards in time, so the individual human life has meanings and significance which point outwards towards the social setting. We can experience this, and it seems at least somewhat plausible to suppose that it can play a part in our evaluation of what is worthwhile in a society.

I should stress how very provisional and speculative much of this is. It cannot serve as anything like a refutation of the utilitarian answer of 'Yes' to question (2). But I have to say that objections that others have offered to the utilitarian answer, based as they have been on what I have called 'contemplative' intuitions, seem even weaker and more tentative. It is tempting simply to regard the question as one that cannot be answered with any degree of confidence. But anyone who has experienced a social order, or some smaller social group, that was unusually harmonious or unharmonious knows the impulse to claim (on the basis of such experience) that the whole can be better, or worse, than the sum of its parts. Applied to the question of value, this gives reason to doubt the utilitarian answer to (2).

3   There is one argument in favour of the utilitarian answer to (2) that I have not mentioned. This is that, all things being equal or nearly equal, one reasonably tends to give answers that will support rather than undermine a generally workable theory. Also, problems in one part of a theory can be dealt with by adjustments in other parts. Whatever might incline us to think that the value in a society is more or less than the sum of individual values might (conceivably) be dealt with by

means of adjustments in how we reckon individual values to be summed.

All of this can reasonably be said also in favour of the utilitarian answer to (3). It is, in my opinion, the reason why great philosophers have accepted this answer. As my arguments in Part Three in favour of the consequentialist component of utilitarianism should suggest, utilitarianism, even in its classical form, is more enlightening and useful than any rival. Why undermine or needlessly complicate a good theory?

The argument that follows will be that not all things are equal or nearly equal with regard to question (3). The answer, I think, has to be 'No'. But I shall try to explain why an answer of 'Yes' would seem attractive.

One reason is this. Utilitarians have wanted a readily usable theory. This means not only one that would meet the strong set of expectations discussed earlier, but also a theory that would have a very wide appeal, based on its capturing fundamental aspects of human experience. The experiences that lead one to attach a positive value to satisfactions and a negative value to dissatisfactions are very fundamental and widely shared indeed, and run through life from the earliest years.

Satisfaction is a genus of which there are many species. Pleasures are satisfactions. There are physical sensations of various kinds that are enjoyed, and which we speak of as pleasures, although pleasures are not physically localised in quite the way that pains can be. (Even someone whose leg is being massaged would not say 'I have a pleasure in my leg'.) There are other pleasures, such as those associated with good friends and good books, whose occurrence is less closely connected with specific physiological stimulation. There are other experiences or states of being to which we attach a positive value that we either would not or would hesitate to call pleasures. The state of not being bothered when one wants time alone to think fits in this category. So does, for many people, the activity of thinking clearly and hard about a challenging problem. For some this brings with it a sense of excitement and uplift that well might incline one to use the word 'pleasure', but for others it is carried on in a calm, even, and matter-of-fact way that makes the word seem slightly out of place. Many of the satisfactions of the 'contemplative life' have for many people a character that makes them not qualify as 'pleasures' in quite the ordinary sense.

'Happiness' is a word that some early utilitarians in some contexts seemed to equate with 'pleasure', although every philosophy student now knows that the two words are not nearly synonymous. The differences, though, are difficult to analyse. One is temporal: we tend to speak of pleasures and pains in relation to short periods of time, and of happiness and unhappiness in relation to longer periods, although people sometimes do speak of having experienced a brief moment of happiness. Another difference, which is more fundamental, concerns the object of satisfaction in the two cases. To feel pleasure is to feel satisfaction at something here and now (or to feel something here and now that is satisfying), even though the object of satisfaction may be itself a thought that refers to the past, the future, or to a considerable period of time. One might feel pleasure at the thought that the Ice Age is past, or that one's declining years will be spent in comfort. It is true that one can be happy at the thought that the Ice Age is past, etc., but to be happy *simpliciter* requires that one be satisfied (at this stage at least) with one's life. Even a moment of happiness implies satisfaction with more than just the sensations of a moment. One must be satisfied with one's life at that moment: anything one is deeply dissatisfied with must either be transformed or excluded from one's sense of the character of one's life at the moment. Thus a mark of the difference between pleasure and happiness is that someone who is in general not satisfied with her or his life can yet experience pleasure (by eating good food, taking refreshing showers, etc.), but can experience happiness only by being satisfied with her or his life. Happiness thus seems a more global kind of satisfaction than pleasure.

There are special difficulties connected with 'happiness': as John Stuart Mill observed, a being of higher faculties requires more to make him happy, so that (even leaving to the side the importance of the 'higher pleasures') Socrates dissatisfied will have more satisfactions in his life than will a satisfied pig. Both 'happiness' and 'pleasure' also turn out to be less precise terms than some philosophers would want to use in a theory designed to meet the strong set of expectations. Also, neither manages clearly to include all kinds of satisfactions. It is arguable indeed that the early utilitarians did mean to claim that all kinds of satisfaction are valuable, but that they used words like 'pleasure' and 'happiness' partly because they wanted to reach a general audience with familiar and untechnical language. Had they used a phrase like 'satisfaction of preferences' for what is valuable, their account perhaps would have been more precise as well as more comprehensive. One thing that suggests a gain in precision is that it is often easier to see whether someone's preference has been satisfied than whether that person is pleased as a result. For public policy makers to ascertain people's preferences might seem more cut and dried, and thereby manageable, than for them to investigate what gives people pleasure or makes them happy.

Whether or not a utilitarianism that generally values satisfaction of preferences (and only satisfaction of preferences) captures the original spirit of utilitarianism, I take it to be characteristic of utilitarianism that satisfactions are what is valued: either satisfactions generically, or some species of satisfactions. On this view, any consequentialist theory that is coupled with a different set of values would not qualify as utilitarianism.

This assuredly is not to say that all positions which do qualify as utilitarian are entirely alike. Among the differences among utilitarian accounts of value, one is especially important and should be noted here. It justifies us in speaking of a strong utilitarian account of value and a weak utilitarian account. The weak utilitarian account is much more plausible, but also less simple. In my argument I shall attack first the strong account and then the weak one.

The strong utilitarian account of value includes the following.

1 All satisfactions (or satisfactions of some specific kind) and only these satisfactions are of value.
2 All dissatisfactions (or dissatisfactions of some specific kind) and only these dissatisfactions are of negative value.
3 Beyond the presence or absence of satisfactions and dissatisfactions (or satisfactions or dissatisfactions of some specific kind), all that matters for value is their intensity or quantity (or the intensity of the preferences that are or are not satisfied).

The weak utilitarian account of value includes (1) and (2) above but not (3). John Stuart Mill immediately comes to mind as someone who endorsed the weak utilitarian account. He argued that 'higher pleasures' are, apart from quantity, worth more than 'lower pleasures'. Thus, in his view, quality of satisfaction mattered as well as quantity or intensity. Presumably someone could hold a weak utilitarian view of value which assigned weight to yet other features of satisfactions. Indeed, it looks as if there is a virtually unlimited range of possible weak utilitarian accounts of value; in comparison, strong utilitarian accounts seem much like one another.

A great virtue of Mill's discussion of 'higher' and 'lower' pleasures is that he was willing to make discriminations based on experience. It is by no means clear that all the judges he considered qualified would endorse his higher rating of the 'higher' pleasures, but his appeal to the comparative judgements of qualified people is a step in the right direction. There is one respect in which the argument is liable to misunderstanding. Mill is not suggesting that any of us would prefer, or should lead, a life in which there are few or no 'lower' pleasures. Rather one can take him to be saying that, in a well balanced life that includes both 'higher' and 'lower' pleasures, 'higher' pleasures will be prized more than 'lower' pleasures of equal strength and intensity. They will be the high points of such a life. 'Higher' pleasures frequently are psychologically strenuous, and thus human limitations ensure that none of our lives will be directed almost entirely towards them. We can seek and enjoy 'lower' pleasures while valuing 'higher' pleasures more.

The strong utilitarian account is appealing in two ways. First, it gives promise of a simpler and more precise theory than Mill could offer, and thus refuses to surrender the strong set of expectations for what an ethical theory should be like. This is attractive, but of course what is promised may be unrealistic. A second kind of appeal is harder to dismiss entirely. An account of value like Mill's, or like the one that I shall endorse finally, is elitist in the sense that it insists on the possibility of outside judgement on what people consider satisfactory or unsatisfactory, so that finally some people's satisfactions (and, by implication, their lives) are considered better than others. This goes very much against the grain in a democratic society; one might even have a sense that it is all right to think such things, but not to say them. Furthermore, it is genuinely dangerous. Once one begins to discriminate amongst satisfactions (or, even worse, declare some to be valueless), then there are risks of encouraging snobbery, envy, unfairness to certain groups, and perhaps even of rationalising exploitation under the guise of preferential treatment for those whose satisfactions are most valuable. Thus there is a strong case for saying that utilitarianism that includes the strong account of value is a much safer (as well as more usable) theory than utilitarianism that includes a weak account of value, or than consequentialism of the sort that I shall endorse.

There is a separate point, which has to do with respect for persons. I am assuming here that respect for persons will be considered important by any reasonable theory: utilitarians certainly can place weight on it in much the way in which Mill placed weight on liberty. Respect for persons tells us that in many contexts it is rude to slight someone else's values, and that in our social behaviour and in public policy decisions it is generally important to treat everyone's preferences as equally worthy of satisfaction. Certain limits to this are recognised: we do not give weight to preferences which require criminal acts, nor do we always give full weight to the preferences of children, and I will argue that respect for persons does not exclude giving preferences for medieval music disproportionate weight (in relation to the preferences of people now alive, and those likely to be alive in the future) in allocating government support for the arts, and that it does not exclude giving preferences for pop music disproportionately little weight. But even in this area respect for persons can affect our conduct: we may despise the music of Lawrence Welk but yet direct people who like it to the store where Lawrence Welk records are being sold.

What I am suggesting is that, on the basis of a wide variety of ethical views including my own, it can be argued that in social practice we ought to treat people's preferences (within the limits and with the minor qualifications just indicated) *as if* they were equally worthy of satisfaction. Thus a utilitarianism that includes the strong account of value may well be approximately correct as an account of how social policy and social behaviour ought to be directed. Let me concede this, but insist that there is a difference between saying that we should act *as if* people's preferences are equally worthy of satisfaction and saying that everyone's preferences *are* equally worthy of satisfaction. This difference might be alleged (dismissively) to be purely theoretical, affecting only the value component of our theory. But this is wrong: the difference is also practical in an important way. Not all of our actions and choices fall within the realm of social behaviour: we must make choices that relate almost entirely to the person we are to be and to which satisfactions we think the most worth attaining. Let us suppose that we believe that Aristotle was right about the contemplative life but we also respect other people's preferences. Then our political decisions and our behaviour in co-operative social ventures might approximate to those to be expected from someone who takes the strong utilitarian position. But our own projects, how we direct our energies, and how we spend our free time, all may be deeply affected by our agreement with Aristotle. A rejection of the strong utilitarian account of value thus has more than theoretical implications.

The most telling argument against the strong utilitarian account of value is a variant of Mill's. We know from experience that not all satisfactions, even given equal strength or intensity, are of equal value. This on the face of it conflicts with some strong utilitarian accounts but not with all. It may be said that, if we value 'higher' pleasures more, this amounts to a stronger preference for them, and that thus Mill's argument does not conflict with a strong utilitarian account of value which claims that all satisfactions of preferences of equal strength are of equal value. In our own lives, the satisfactions that we value more will correspond to preferences that are stronger.

This last may or may not be true. It is arguable that we find certain kinds of experiences more valuable than we had expected (and than is mirrored in the strength of our original preferences), and other kinds less valuable. Also it is arguable that something like weakness of will can lead to a strong preference for something that a person considers to be of slight value. But, even putting both of these points to the side, we can see one strong objection to the strong utilitarian account that proportions value to strength of preference. This is that, in viewing other people's lives, we can reasonably judge that it is intrinsically more valuable that some slight or non-existent preferences be satisfied than that some strong preferences be satisfied.

Let us suppose that someone has shown herself to be highly intelligent and to possess great latent sensitivity, but that this person also greatly enjoys sunbathing and long periods of mindless relaxation. As we remarked earlier, even a very well directed life has plenty of room for such things as sunbathing and mindless relaxation; but let us suppose that this person wishes to make these the centre of her life. (We may assume also that this is a considered preference that would survive cognitive psychotherapy.) It is open to us to judge that the life which would result if she pursued more regularly her occasional slight preferences for study and for exposure to the arts would be intrinsically better, whether or not it would provide more satisfactions or more intense satisfactions, than the life which would result if she pursued her stronger preference for days spent entirely in relaxation. In other words, the life she prefers may be intrinsically less worth living than another that is available to her. It is widely agreed that people's strongest preferences are not necessarily for what is most in their interests. In some cases, this is demonstrable because of dissatisfaction that people come to feel after they have got what they wanted. In other cases, we judge that people have made the wrong choice even if they are very satisfied afterwards. This is true of the inhabitants of Huxley's Brave New World and of the Land of the Lotus Eaters described in the *Odyssey*. We commonly judge that some satisfactions are inferior to others even if the people in whose lives they occur judge differently.

Thus an argument like Mill's, which appeals to the judgements of value that would be made by people who have experienced (or can imaginatively reconstruct), and remain capable of, a variety of satisfactions has great strength even against the strong utilitarian account which proportions value to strength of preference. The argument is supported both by the sense that many of us have of what is valuable, and also by the kinds of judgements that we commonly consider it reasonable to make.

Mill leaves us with a complicated utilitarianism, in which possibilities for measurement (to the extent that there ever were any) are blunted by the fact that we must take into account quality as well as quantity of satisfaction. Are there reasons to go further away from the strong utilitarian account?

My suggestion is that, once we agree that the satisfaction of some preferences can be worth intrinsically rather little in comparison to the satisfaction of others (even holding intensity of preference and of satisfaction constant), then it is difficult not to take the further step of saying that the satisfaction of some preferences is intrinsically worth nothing, or less than nothing. Consider someone's preference for torturing young children. (This could be a considered preference; whether it could survive cognitive psychotherapy is open to debate.) It may be difficult to arrive at a fair evaluation of this, because of the great repugnance that almost everyone has for sadism, especially sadism in which the victims are innocent and unusually defenceless. And of course, in estimating *intrinsic* value, we must put to the side the suffering of the victims and other bad effects. Utilitarians strongly condemn sadism, because the suffering it produces and other bad effects so greatly outweigh the comparatively small value assigned to the sadist's satisfaction; our question is whether this small value should be assigned, rather than zero or a negative value. Bearing all of this in mind, we can I think arrive at a fair estimate of the intrinsic value of the sadist's satisfactions by imaginatively reconstructing what it would be to have this kind of preference and to feel pleasure from its satisfaction. It seems to me that, judging it dispassionately, we can arrive at a sense that this kind of satisfaction is intrinsically of negative value: that apart from its effects on the rest of one's life or on others it is worse to feel this kind of satisfaction than to be in a dreamless sleep or a coma. The following thought experiment may help the reader. Suppose that at some point you have a choice between spending the remaining years of your life in a coma and spending these years engrossed by the illusion (to be made convincing by hypnotic suggestion) of inflicting tortures on young children combined with the pleasure and other responses typically had by extreme sadists. Surely the former is preferable. If this is correct, then we have to conclude that the traditional utilitarian account of value is unacceptable, in that some satisfactions are not of positive intrinsic value.

One line of defence that is available to a utilitarian is as follows. The utilitarian can concede that some satisfactions are of no value, but can still maintain something that resembles utilitarianism on the basis of this assertion: that nothing is valuable that does not include satisfaction. Satisfaction, in other words, can be claimed to be a necessary condition of value even if it is not a sufficient one. In this way, the characteristic utilitarian link between value and satisfaction is preserved.

There is perhaps some truth to the claim that satisfaction is a necessary condition for value, if the period of life evaluated is long enough. A life totally devoid of satisfactions is, to say the least, seriously flawed. Something – some touch of sweetness – is missing, but also we might well have reason to question the character of the person who leads such a life: as Aristotle points out, the exercise of virtues carries with it pleasure. Even old blind Oedipus reported satisfaction with his own character.

There are episodes, though, such as those in which someone is entirely busy in fighting hard in a lost good cause, in which dissatisfactions can engross the consciousness of even a virtuous person. People sometimes look back on such episodes and take satisfaction in them: in the fact that one did one's best; perhaps also in the camaraderie with others on the same side. This retrospective satisfaction, though, does not obscure the fact that in some cases one's thoughts at the time were full of dissatisfaction. The retrospective satisfaction is a favourable judgement, but it is one assuredly not based on satisfactions felt at the time. This suggests strongly that we judge some episodes to be of value despite the absence of satisfactions. They might have been better had there been satisfactions, but that is beside the point. The point is that, at least for short periods of time, satisfaction is not a necessary condition for value.

Neither is it true that dissatisfaction is a necessary condition for negative value: the case of the very satisfied sadist shows this. It might seem more plausible to hold that dissatisfaction is a sufficient condition for negative value. But the dissatisfactions of someone engrossed in fighting in a lost good cause show that this is not the case. We would, it is true, judge it intrinsically better that the preferences of such a person be satisfied. But, if a man's preference to take drugs is frustrated, and instead he reads poetry (which he only mildly likes or is indifferent to) while feeling dissatisfaction at not getting his drugs, we might well judge that the experience that includes dissatisfaction at not getting what he wanted was intrinsically better than would have been the experience that would have included satisfaction at getting what he wanted.

In sum I have outlined a case for denying all of the following: (1) that all satisfactions (or all pleasures) are of intrinsic value, (2) that only satisfactions (or pleasures) are of intrinsic value, (3) that all dissatisfactions are of negative intrinsic value, and (4) that only dissatisfactions are of negative value. (In relation to the view that what is valuable is the satisfaction of preferences that would survive cognitive psychotherapy, the case is more complicated. My own view is that sadistic preferences had by a very clever and manipulative person could survive cognitive psychotherapy, although they might be modified and watered down in the process. But in any event my main argument implies that, even if it is the case that satisfaction of preferences that would survive cognitive psychotherapy always has some intrinsic value, it is not the case that only satisfaction of such preferences has intrinsic value. An episode in which a man's preference for sunning himself on the beach is thwarted and instead he has to engage in the frustrating activity of thinking about philosophy can yet have intrinsic value.)

The case rests ultimately on judgements of value that many of us are in a position to make. This foundation perhaps is not as firm as one would like: there is no reason to assume that all competent judges will agree. But neither is the foundation as flimsy as some might suggest. We do customarily distinguish cases in which someone is in a good position to make a judgement of value from cases in which someone is in a poor position, and, as the philosophical literature on the subject of values testifies, there are broad areas of recurrent widespread agreement among people who are in a position to make the appropriate judgements. In our culture from Plato and Aristotle on, and in the 'wisdom' literature of other cultures, there are, amongst all the differences, broad recurrent similarities. I shall discuss some grounds for caution about generalisations shortly, but the areas of agreement about the high intrinsic value of psychological harmony and of demanding forms of aesthetic and intellectual activity, and the judgement made within many traditions that some satisfactions are valueless, deserve mention. These add additional weight to the case against the utilitarian account of value.

Having argued against this account, we can ask, 'What *is* of value?' With what are we to replace the utilitarian account of value? Part of the answer is G.E. Moore's, that the final truth is that a great many different kinds of things have intrinsic value. The final chapter of *Principia Ethica* might perhaps be faulted for emphasising passive and contemplative experiences at the expense of active and creative, and for inadequate attention to the foundational values of psychological harmony which Plato especially had emphasised. Experiences that have value, after all, take place in the context of an individual's sense of herself or himself. But Moore's account remains a valuable corrective to doctrinaire views of value.

Anyone who wants an account of value much more systematic and precise than this must be disappointed. Let us bear in mind the following. We pointed out earlier that someone of wisdom and wide experience who has experienced something in a sustained way is in an optimal position to be confident of a value judgement of it. Very commonly, however, people judge the value not only of what they have experienced but also of things thought to be like what they have experienced. It is normal to extrapolate from the value of what we have experienced to that of something slightly different. In fact we do not expect that any two people will have exactly the same experiences, or that our own experiences will entirely repeat themselves, so that if talk about values is to have any use it must be at least somewhat general. The danger is that other people's experience (or our own future experience) may differ significantly from what we have had in ways that are masked by the broad labels that we use, and that this may vitiate our generalisations. A value judgement based on experience can be badly founded if the difference between what was experienced and what is judged is significant. Thus value generalisations must always be taken as problematic.

This should be understood as indicating the need for caution and recurrent scepticism, and not as indicating that we cannot arrive at useful generalisations about values experienced by different persons. First, we must realise that some aspects of human experience seem to be more closely shared than are others. The experience of not having enough to eat, or of being in constant physical pain, no doubt varies slightly from person to person, and from culture to culture; but there is a great deal to suggest that there are more similarities than differences.

The core of traditional morality, indeed, consists of prohibitions on inflicting experiences judged to be of great negative value; and these do appear very generally to be of great negative value. Thus, if we are to worry about value generalisations, those connected with general rules at the core of traditional morality are most secure. The same can be said about the value generalisations connected with the most urgent issues of public policy, concerned with such matters as the relief of poverty and disease.

Also it is possible to recognise that a number of items, to which we would apply the same broad label, vary a great deal in character and value, and still to make useful value generalisations (of an imprecise kind) about them. Take for example G.E. Moore's claim that the experience of affection for a person worthy of it is of high value. We know that conventions of love and affection vary from culture to culture, and that affection has different cultural roles and degrees of importance. So what we call affection will not, in its various manifestations, fit any precise formula; neither will it always have exactly the same value. But this does not prevent us from seeing that Moore's claim is right, as a rough generalisation, with modifications and adjustments perhaps to be made for specific cases. In much the same way, Aristotle's highly favourable evaluation of the contemplative life can be held to have a rough general correctness, even if anything that could be called a contemplative life in classical China or in Modern America might differ significantly from what Aristotle had in mind. Other rough generalisations can be made about the value of personal autonomy, creative activity, variety of experience, peace of mind, etc. That these have to be treated cautiously is no reason for not making them. Indeed, because human experiences do have their similarities and recurrent patterns, value generalisations can be useful guides to others in their private pursuits as well as having use in discussions of social policy.

It should be said, finally, that even if utilitarianism is wrong about the value of satisfaction, it is not far wrong. The most primitive and widely shared experience of value is of the negative value of pain and frustration and of the positive value (with exceptions already noted) of pleasure and fulfilment. Any account of value which does not acknowledge this runs the risk of being (in the bad sense of the word) a mandarin view. Furthermore, even a highly developed life is lacking something if it does not include a great number (and a variety) of satisfactions, or if it includes too many frustrations and pains. All of us of course lead lives that include a mixture of satisfactions and frustrations. If one hypothesises a human life with no frustrations whatsoever, one imagines a life devoid of excitement and of challenges, in which the attainment of psychologically strenuous satisfactions is unlikely. Thus a modicum of frustration has an instrumental value in promoting certain kinds of satisfaction. But very few lives run the risk of including too many satisfactions and not enough frustrations. The experience had by Socrates dissatisfied is presumed preferable to that enjoyed by a satisfied pig, but the experience had by Socrates satisfied must be deemed preferable to both.

NOTES AND REFERENCES

Richard Brandt's discussion of cognitive psychotherapy as a value-free reflection is to be found in *A Theory of the Good and the Right* (Oxford, 1979), pp. 111–13. Some discussion of Brandt is to be found in my 'Value judgements', *Philosophy and Phenomenological Research*, forthcoming. J.S. Mill's discussion of the 'higher' and 'lower' pleasures is to be found in *Utilitarianism*, pp. 12–15 of the Bobbs-Merrill edition edited by Oskar Piest. His views about the happiness of philosophers, fools, and pigs are on pp. 13–14. Aristotle's dialectical sorting through judgements of value (and dismissing some as worthless) can be found in the *Nicomachean Ethics*, Book I. His contention that exercise of virtues brings pleasure is in 1104b (pp. 36–8 of the Ostwald translation). G.E. Moore's discussion of the beautiful and ugly unperceived worlds is in *Principia Ethica* (Cambridge, 1903), pp. 83–5. The passage quoted about judgements which are intuitive only in a 'psychological sense' is on pp. 148–9. The claim about the value of affection is on pp. 203–5.

An interesting discussion, different from mine, of the components of utilitarian theory is to be found in Amartya Sen's 'Utilitarianism and welfarism', *Journal of Philosophy*, 1979). My account of the value of a life being not necessarily equal to the sum of the values of its parts may seem to imply a view of personal identity opposed to that found in, for example, *The Questions of King Milinda*, trans. T.W. Rhys Davids (Delhi, 1969), or Derek Parfit, 'Personal identity' (*Philosophical Review*, 1971). However, I take there not to be a fundamental opposition: my assumption is merely that the life of a person, whatever its fundamental reality is, is normally experienced as a somewhat integrated whole. I do go on to suggest, in effect, that the value of a whole whose parts we normally would assign to different lives also is not necessarily equal to the sum of the values of the parts.

Just after the text of this chapter was completed, Professor R.M. Hare was kind enough to send me a copy of the proofs of his forthcoming book, *Moral Thinking*. *Moral Thinking* is a major achievement, and it makes it clear that Professor Hare would not agree with my main conclusions in this chapter. I do think, however, that my arguments in the chapter can stand as they are; and I judge that detailed comment on *Moral Thinking* would be out of place here, although I shall supply some in a piece on 'Utilitarianism Today' that has been commissioned by *Revue Internationale de Philosophie*. The reader is urged to consult *Moral Thinking*, especially Chapter 5, for a tightly argued alternative to the view argued in this chapter.

Part Three
The Case for Consequentialism

Chapter 7

First Pattern of Argument

To many people the objections to utilitarianism developed in the last chapter will not seem the most serious that can be raised. I did suggest that in social practice (which includes public policy decisions, and in general all or almost all moral decisions) we should act (with some qualifications) as if the satisfaction of preferences of equal intensity is of equal value: in other words, that something approximating to utilitarianism gives a correct account of how we should behave towards other people. All in all, it may be said, I have not deviated very far from utilitarianism.

In any event, the most vehement opposition to utilitarianism has not been concerned primarily with the utilitarian account of values. Rather, the consequentialist component of utilitarianism has been most under attack. In this section I will argue that some form of consequentialism is correct. Further, I will specify what form is correct, and will explain how it is to be conjoined with the account of value given in the previous chapter to form a complete theory. The reader then can judge to what extent this theory approximates, or deviates from, utilitarianism.

Three patterns of argument will be given. The first, in this chapter, is defensive in character. I will show that objections to consequentialism that are often urged can take a plausible form only if they themselves rest on consequentialist considerations. This will amount to a recursive argument for consequentialism: namely that consequentialism at some level of theory can be plausibly objected to only if it is introduced at a more fundamental level.

My argument will be first of all for the following.

> *Proposition C*   In any case in which it is not true that one should do what has the best consequences, the reason for this has to be based on some judgement of consequences.

In this, and in subsequent discussion, it is assumed that the term 'consequences of X' means the set which includes X itself and physical and psychological events that are concomitant with, or follow from, X; it is assumed also (as part of the characteristic consequentialist treatment of consequences) that in no form of consequentialism can a particular consequence automatically override all others or be given

infinite weight. Proposition C is the claim that some form of consequentialism is correct, that the only valid reason for not doing what
has the best consequences (understood with the stipulations just
mentioned) is that the act in question is ruled out by some moral rule,
policy, motive, or system of attitudes which itself is shown to be
desirable by virtue of its consequences (understood with the stipulations just mentioned).

In arguing for Proposition C, we must not lose sight of the real world
to which it is meant to be applied. In real life we are never sure of what
all the consequences will be of actions that are open to us. We also may
not be entirely sure of what the alternatives are that are open to us. As
a number of writers have pointed out, there is a kind of moral creativity
in difficult situations that consists in thinking of alternatives besides
the obvious ones. All of this is worth bearing in mind. It shows that
consequentialism, in any form, is far less precise, and far more difficult
to apply, than it may seem. This does not mean, however, that consequentialism can never be applied or that it is so vague as to be
useless. In real life we may make rough non-quantitative judgements
of degrees of importance, and we may balance prospective gains (for
others and for ourselves) against risks. Later I shall argue that consequentialism, even conjoined with the complicated and imprecise
account of values given in the previous chapter, constitutes a usable
and useful theory.

Consequentialist policies, of various sorts, can be pursued in the face
of uncertainty and imprecision; but they make sense only if some
general consequentialist proposition, statable without reference to
uncertainty and imprecision, is correct. It makes sense to balance
prospective gains against risks only if there is some correct general
proposition about doing what has the best consequences in the ab-
stracted and unreal case in which we know what has the best consequences. Let us begin then with the simplest, and seemingly most
straightforward, consequentialist proposition.

> *Proposition AC*   One should always do what has the best con-
> sequences.

There are a number of factors that give Proposition AC immediate
plausibility, besides its generality and simplicity. It advocates acting
responsibly: instead of adopting the attitude of 'I made a moral choice;
it fell to earth I know not where', one adopts the attitude of caring
about the results of one's actions. Further, if something (happiness,
satisfaction of desires, or moral virtue) is of value, there is an obvious
point in bringing about as much of it as is possible. Proposition AC also
has the virtue of giving us at least some independence from cultural
biases and indoctrination: instead of basing our morality on a received

First Pattern / 95

vision of what is 'fitting' (for example what used to be perceived as the fittingness of the poor deferring to the wealthy), we have a chance to arrive at a more matter-of-fact morality which rests on observation of how certain practices actually work.

Why then should we not simply seek to do what has the best consequences? There are two main lines of objection to Proposition AC.

> *Objection 1*   To accept AC and to try to lead one's life on its basis would be to opt for an undesirable personal character. Therefore AC is to be rejected.
> *Objection 2*   In some cases the alternative that has the best consequences happens to be morally wrong. Therefore AC is to be rejected.

Each of these objections to AC has three especially attractive or likely forms. Thus we can examine six forms of objection to AC, as follows.

O1a   To accept AC and to try to lead one's life on its basis would be to be an excessively calculating and unspontaneous person.

O1b   To follow AC would be to feel one's policies and commitments as more provisional than should be the case for a decent, reliable person.

O1c   To follow AC would be to be, first and foremost, altruistic. But it is better (more satisfying, more estimable) to be independent and oriented towards personal projects than to be an altruist. Everyone should look out for, first and foremost, himself or herself.

O2a   What AC recommends in some cases is wrong, in that some of its recommendations violate valid moral rules.

O2b   What AC recommends in some cases is wrong, in that some of its recommendations call for an agent to violate the rights of others.

O2c   What AC recommends in some cases is wrong, full stop: the wrongness is, as it were, intrinsic, and does not need to be derived from moral rules or from statements that certain rights are not to be violated.

Let us discuss *O1a* first. A *locus classicus* for this objection is a philosophical joke, told by John Rawls. Jeremy Bentham says, 'When I run to the other wicket after my partner has struck a good ball I do so because it is best on the whole.' An act consequentialist (someone who accepts Proposition AC) might reasonably reply with the story of Isaac Newton, who, asked why he had been hit on the head by a ball while playing in the field, replied with an exposition of the Law of Gravity. In both physics and ethics, it might be said, to account for everyday and easy cases by direct reference to fundamental and abstract laws is not only unnecessary but also comically pompous. There is, however, a difference between the cases of Bentham and Newton. It is clear that Newton does not have to be constantly mindful of the Law of Gravity in order to be governed by it; this is open to question in the case of Bentham and the Utilitarian Principle. But a consequentialist can reasonably say, as J.J.C. Smart has, that the policy of not thinking about consequences during normal sporting activity (and presumably during other kinds of normal everyday activity) has good consequences and on that account is to be adopted.

The point is that *O1a* can rest on an appeal to consequences: the undesirable consequences for one's own spontaneity of keeping something like AC in mind. There is only one way in which *O1a* can emerge as a non-consequentialist objection to AC. That is if the objector maintains that it is better to be spontaneous than constantly to think of consequences, even if the bad consequences for others of one's spontaneity outweigh any good consequences for oneself. To advocate this is to advocate what we customarily term irresponsibility: most of us who believe in the value of spontaneity in fact customarily distinguish areas of life in which the effects of our actions on others are not likely to be serious enough to outweigh the value of spontaneity from other areas in which this is not the case. When we become aware that some of our actions have serious consequences, we normally consider it appropriate to reflect on them. Jeremy Bentham will reflect on the greatest good of the greatest number, after his partner has struck a good ball, if the opposing bowler has threatened suicide. Someone who is enjoyably casual and carefree in most situations of life ought to become reflective when his or her actions impinge on the extreme vulnerability of others. It is hard to imagine a human life in which the majority of actions have major effects on others – such a life would be very different from any of ours – but we would hope that such a person would be careful, and not too carefree and spontaneous. To speak as we have been doing of 'irresponsibility' is of course not in itself to prove wrong the non-consequentialist version of *O1a*; it is merely to point out that the only plausible version of *O1a* is a consequentialist one. And this is what our argument requires.

Let us now consider *O1b*. This represents the inside view of the point made by those who ask, 'Who would take seriously a promise made by a consequentialist?' Consequentialists sometimes attempt to meet this point (to be discussed more fully in relation to *O2a*) by pointing to the side-effects of breaking promises, violating commitments, or letting down those who depend on one. There are likely bad effects on one's future attitudes and behaviour, on personal relationships, and on the general atmosphere of trust some degree of which is necessary to society. These side-effects are often so significant that, if a philosopher asks about a case in which a net of 1,000 units of good (mainly for a promisee) would be brought about by keeping a promise, and a net of 1,001 units of good would be brought about by breaking a promise, one knows that in this case some major harm would be prevented (or good brought about) by breaking the promise, in order to bring about even a slight surplus. The philosopher has neglected to say what this major factor is, and until it is specified we are in no position to make a judgement.

Nevertheless there is something to be said for this general line of attack on AC. It is widely recognised that promises ought to be broken if keeping them will bring about serious harm, or will prevent great good; and in this sense commitments in general are not inviolable. But there is something unsettling about being associated with people who are in a state of readiness to break commitments, and it should be even more unsettling to be such a person. A consequentialist can recognise this. There are good consequences attached to having an attitude of not thinking about the consequences of keeping one's commitments, except in extreme circumstances. Thus there is a very plausible consequentialist form of *O1b*.

Is there a plausible non-consequentialist form? There is general agreement that, on the whole, fidelity to one's commitments has good consequences. It is hard to imagine what a world would be like in which this was not true. Thus any result of a thought experiment involving a world in which keeping commitments had generally poor consequences would be unreliable. The harder it is to imagine details of a world, or of a situation, the poorer our position to judge what would be appropriate in it.

Given the fact that any world we can adequately imagine will be one in which fidelity to commitments has in general good consequences, we can ask whether it is because of these good consequences that we value fidelity. There are familiar arguments, to be found in Hume and Mill, that our immediate sense of what is appropriate in such matters is derivable from our general preference for the useful. What is the alternative? The major alternative is that there is some logical power in a commitment, or in a moral rule governing commitments, which accounts for the fact that it is a virtue to take one's promises and other commitments very seriously. Our discussion of moral rules in Chapter 2, however, has revealed the absence of anything like such a logical power. The non-consequentialist version of *O1b* must therefore be considered implausible.

O1c raises different problems. This line of objection to AC represents a moderate egoism. Much philosophical ink has been spilled about the more extreme forms of egoism, but they are not represented here: arguably they are not moral views, but rather the refusal to enter into moral reflection or judgement at all. There is no arguing with a person who says simply 'I want what I want'; such a person may mimic the terminology of moral discussion, and say 'My interests ought to be considered above everyone else's'; but we can agree with Hume that to make a genuine moral judgement is to make an implicit appeal for the agreement of others (an appeal which thus must rest on impersonally statable considerations), and with Hare that moral judgements are subject to the logical requirement of universalisability. The moderate egoism of $O1c$ passes these tests.

One can consistently, of course, prefer one's own interests to those of others as long as one accords the same right to others (except, perhaps, in cases in which there are relevant differences). It is frequently pointed out, indeed, that some policy along these lines will have better consequences than a policy of single-minded, continuous altruism. We are much better equipped, the argument runs, to look out for our own interests than to look out for those of others; indeed, others may not always appreciate our unflinching concern. This leads to a common-sense policy which many people would assent to: one looks out for one's own interests first, and assumes that others will do likewise, but in cases in which actions look likely to have major effects on the well-being of others one's policy is to try to give everyone's interests equal weight.

There are two difficulties with this. One is that it is no longer possible (if it ever was) to seal off areas of life in which one's actions have a drastic effect on others from other areas. One always could be doing more to help famine victims in poor countries: as Jonathan Glover points out, even the decision to read a novel or buy a concert ticket is a decision not to spend the time working for (or not to donate the money to) Oxfam. This suggests that some forms of consequentialism, including classical utilitarianism, might entail a very heavy moral burden on us.

A second, independent, difficulty is that, even if we maintain some shred of a distinction between areas of life in which our actions have some major direct, immediate, and visible effect on others and areas in which our actions do not, it is not clear that in the former areas one can be expected to give everyone's interests entirely equal weight. This was discussed in Chapter 3, in relation to Andrew Oldenquist's example of one's own child and another child drowning nearby. Even in the important moral choice of which child to save first, impartiality is not entirely in place, although, as I suggested earlier, it is not entirely out of place either.

What this suggests is a familiar truth. We commonly organise our sense of responsibility so that we feel more responsible to family and friends than to strangers, to those nearby than to those far away. We do not commonly give everyone's interests exactly equal weight, even in important matters. At the centre of most people's concern is themselves, and even well-meaning people consider it proper to give their own interests preference even in some situations in which the results for others will be important. An example would be the case in which two people are competing for a job, and the loser will be unemployed, or the case in which two people are competing for an attractive marriage partner and the loser will be depressed and lonely.

There is a consequentialist solution to both difficulties. One has to choose attitudes and policies with an eye to consequences, and in reckoning consequences we must take into account human psychology, and especially our own psychology. Most of us are capable of more self-denial than we exercise, but few of us have an infinite capacity. Consequentialist policies have to be workable over the long haul, which means that they can ask only what can be sustained. But we must carefully limit the context, and also the degree of preference. We may think it right that a man save his child before another, but wrong if he saves his child from injury before saving another from death, and wrong also if he gives the child preference in a banking or hiring decision. It seems appropriate for people to compete freely for jobs or for marriage partners, but there are cases in which we might judge that competition for scarce resources such as food ought to be limited.

The phrase that comes to mind is 'the rules of the game': standards for when and how it is appropriate to pursue one's private interest or to favour the interests of those with whom one is connected. The present rules of the game may work badly, as in the Jean Renoir film with that title; and it is important that they be open to criticism. In particular, even if it is useful (in terms of presenting manageable moral burdens, and also encouraging the development and play of human affections) that people generally adopt policies of favouring the interests of their families and friends over the interests of people far away, it can be argued that the consequences of these policies would be better if the interests of those who are far away were not so heavily discounted as they tend to be at present. A similar point can be made about the interests of animals. And no doubt other criticisms of the present moral conventions can be made.

All of this will be discussed further in Chapter 11. The present point is that a consequentialist can consistently maintain (a) that it is useful for us to make a rough distinction between moments and occasions in which we are highly accountable for the effects of our actions on others and moments in which we are not, and (b) that it is useful for us to adopt policies that encourage some degree of preference (in some circumstances) for our own interests and the interests of those close to us. A consequentialist can maintain that some ways of drawing the line between the self-regarding and other-regarding parts of our lives have better consequences than others, and thus are to be preferred; a consequentialist can make a similar claim about some policies circumscribing the kind and degree of preference for our own interests (or the interests of those close to us) as opposed to others, and thus is not committed to endorsing the policies actually followed by most decent and well-meaning people nowadays. This is to say that the objection to AC under discussion can be given a very plausible consequentialist basis. If a policy of continuous single-minded altruism is impossible for the very great majority of people to sustain, and if it would tend to deprive people of the motivation for various kinds of achievement, then there are consequentialist reasons for recommending policies that incorporate some degree of moderate egoism.

Are there plausible non-consequentialist grounds for recommending moderate egoism? The most plausible contender might involve removing the burden of proof from moderate egoism, by regarding altruism as a deviation (requiring special justification) from egoism rather than the reverse. This might be done by someone who claims that individual rights provide a justification for pursuing one's own interest which make this kind of behaviour a norm rather than a deviation. We can take this up in our discussion of *O2b*.

Let us now consider the most frequently raised objection, *O2a*. The strong version of this is that AC is immoral because it would lead us to violate valid moral rules. Our discussion in Chapter 2 of moral rules has laid the groundwork for a reply. If familiar moral rules, that thoughtful people will agree are generally valid, have exceptions – unusual cases in which conduct of the kind forbidden by the rule happens to be morally acceptable – then a defender of AC can claim that cases in which AC does conflict with a moral rule are best described as cases in which AC can enable us to discover an exception to the rule. That AC leads to violation of valid moral rules is, in itself, a ground for objection only if we accept rigorism; and rigorism is very implausible.

There is, however, a weaker version of *O2a* which has considerable plausibility. This is that AC would lead to violation of valid moral rules in cases in which they should not be violated, and more generally would lead us to take generally valid moral rules too lightly: that it would make us too ready to search for, and to claim to find, exceptions. This complaint, however, is closely linked to the complaint about the results for personal character of AC that was discussed under *O1b*. A consequentialist can plausibly recommend, on consequentialist grounds, a policy of very great respect for moral rules. It is useful that we respect them, and that we be highly reluctant to violate them. The only way in which a plausible non-consequentialist basis can be provided for such a reluctance would be if we could appeal to an inherent logical power in the rules. But our discussion in Chapter 2 has made clear how little reason there is to postulate such a power. And it seems mysterious to say, on one hand, that we ought to be reluctant to break our promises because of the logical power of the rule that governs promise-keeping, but, on the other hand, admit that the rule, in any form in which we can formulate it, has exceptions.

Let us turn now to *O2b*. It is often said that AC would lead to violations of rights, and it is often said also that the leading rival approaches to ethics today are utilitarian and 'rights-based'. Thus *O2b* must be taken especially seriously; and yet, of course, to be understood it requires some explanation of what a right is, and how rights can be determined.

A standard and illuminating account of the former has been provided by Joel Feinberg, who has explored the conceptual linkage between having a right and being in a position to claim something as one's due. Feinberg points out that 'to think of oneself as the holder of rights is not to be unduly but properly proud, to have that minimal self-respect that is necessary to be worthy of the love and esteem of others'. At this point, anyone, even a consequentialist, may be struck by the beneficial consequences of having rights, so described, recognised and respected within a society. It would appear from the contents of *On Liberty* that Mill, too, was struck by this. Thus it is especially easy to see that there is a plausible consequentialist form of *O2b*: in some cases one should deviate from AC because someone's rights would be violated otherwise, and a general readiness to respect the rights of others has good consequences. The point can be put even more strongly: it has good consequences not to be prepared even to consider violating or waiving someone's rights, except in a case which is clearly extraordinary in which respecting rights carries with it great dangers for others.

Mill conspicuously does not regard the rights he defends as inalienable. They depend on conditions and states of society. Certain freedoms, for example, could not be justified among 'barbarians'. Rights exist in his view only when there is a general consequentialist justification of them. In order to see if there is a plausible non-consequentialist version of *O2b*, we must see whether there are rights that would obtain even when there was no general consequentialist justification for recognising and respecting them. Yet this is less simple than it might appear. Take for example the right to live of a rational being already alive; to make the case even more extreme, we may exclude from the discussion terminally ill people as well as foetuses. Can one imagine in any detail what a society would be like in which it would *not* be generally useful to respect such a right, and what it would be like to function in such a society? This is one of those matters in which 'intuitions' are bound to be unreliable.

Nevertheless we can separate two questions. One concerns how useful it is that people generally have certain inhibitions: that there are certain things that they generally will not do, and even in the extreme cases in which things of that kind are justified will be reluctant to do (and will be regretful about afterwards). The other concerns whether there are certain rights which not only are, as it were, the trump cards in moral decision, but which also are the only trumps, so that they always are decisive. Both consequentialists and non-consequentialists can defend the importance of having strong inhibitions that correlate with recognised human rights. But the consequentialist defence is independent of any view that these rights both are inalienable and never should be waived: even if the rights are alienable, in any state of society we can adequately imagine it will be useful to have strong inhibitions corresponding to them, and perhaps it will be useful not to entertain in advance questions of when it would be appropriate to waive or violate them. The non-consequentialist defence of inhibitions about rights, on the other hand, looks not very plausible unless it is conjoined with a view that the rights both are inalienable and never should be waived. If this view is incorrect, then there is no absolute power possessed by rights; then it is hard to see what ground there is other than the consequentialist one for distinguishing between cases in which we should respect them and cases in which we should not; and it is thus hard to see what ground other than the consequentialist one there is for having strong inhibitions corresponding to rights.

Are there rights that are inalienable and should never be waived? Could one prove either that there are or that there are not? I intend to sidestep this latter question by offering an argument that it is plausible to suppose that there are no rights which both are inalienable and should never be waived. This leaves the field open to anyone who wants to overturn my argument by offering a proof that there are rights which both are inalienable and should never be waived. In the absence of such a proof, though, we will be able to conclude that there is a plausible case for denying that there are rights which both are inalienable and should never be waived, and accordingly that the only plausible ground for *O2b* is the consequentialist one.

The plausible case is as follows. The leading candidates for status as inalienable rights are those mentioned in the American Declaration of Independence: life, liberty, and the pursuit of happiness. Yet within our legal tradition it is recognised that two of these rights, and to some extent the third, may be waived. It is recognised that the state in a time of emergency is justified in depriving certain young men, for the period, of liberty and their chosen means for the pursuit of happiness, and in exposing them to a probability of death which in some cases is very high. That this is widely recognised as being justified does not, of course, establish that it is indeed justified; although a pacifist might well hold that there are imaginable occasions of national danger other than war in which something like selective service would be justified. Even if military selective service is not justified, one might believe that selective service as medical assistants in a time of plague could be justified. What our legal practice in these matters and the moral opinion that supports it do show is that there is a plausible *prima facie* case for saying that under certain circumstances it is justifiable to waive people's rights to liberty and the pursuit of happiness, and to expose them to a high probability of death. Immediate death is never certain, even for the prisoner connected to the electric chair, although 'for practical purposes' it is certain; death can also be 'for practical purposes' certain for those required to participate in certain military or medical activities for which sufficient volunteers are not available. The person who orders someone to advance into a free-fire zone or a plague zone may reasonably have a sense of having caused that person's death, just as the warden's orders cause the death of the condemned prisoner. Again, none of this amounts to a demonstration that the right to life ever should be (in some such way) waived. But it suggests that it is treated in this way in America, and that someone who wanted to argue that it never should be waived would have to begin by attacking both the selective service system and any parallel system that might satisfy a pacifist before going on to lay down a method of showing that rights of some sort both are inalienable and should never be waived.

Virtually no one, of course, holds that there is any right which ought to be respected if a clear result would be the destruction of all or virtually all human life; although specific cases of such a stark choice are bound to sound fanciful, and in any event should not be dwelt upon. (A fascination with extreme cases that provide exceptions is dangerous in that it promotes a tendency to look for exceptions in less extreme cases.) We have already pointed out that there are good consequentialist grounds, outlined by Mill and others, for treating certain rights with very great general respect. It is hard to see what the non-consequentialist grounds would be, especially if it is conceded that there is no right that obtains in all imaginable cases. It is valuable that we recognise rights; but it must be said also that these are the sophisticated modern counterparts of taboos, and perhaps all one is left with, after analysis, is a *feeling* of something glowing with mysterious force. A consequentialist can account for why we do, and should, have this feeling.

Let us return to *O1c* with all of this in mind. Rights frequently are invoked by those who wish to treat moderate egoism as the ethical norm and altruism as the departure that always requires special justification. It is worth pointing out, first of all, that not all appeals to rights have the same character. Many have the function of protecting the unfortunate, downtrodden, or especially vulnerable: appeals to rights made by various United Nations organisations, or by Amnesty International, generally have this character. Some appeals to rights, though, have a very different function, that of protecting people who are not unfortunate, downtrodden, or especially vulnerable from having demands made on them. Let me suggest that these rights, too, have a consequentialist justification, although it is neither as strong or as dramatic as the consequentialist justification for the rights of the first sort. It promotes people's sense of security and stability, and perhaps encourages individual incentive, to recognise certain general rights not to have demands made on one: although I might add that the consequentialist justification may not be for as strong a version of such rights as some people would wish. There may be no consequentialist justification for an alleged right not to be taxed heavily for the benefit of programmes to help the poor. In any event, our argument thus far has shown that the only plausible view of rights of this sort is that any justification they have is consequentialist. This indicates that the only justification for ever not giving equal weight to everyone's interests is consequentialist, and accordingly that the only plausible version of *O1c* is consequentialist.

Let us turn now to *O2c*. This objection inevitably involves the most direct appeal to 'intuition'. The claim is that an action which AC would seem to endorse is in fact wrong, and that it is wrong not because – or perhaps not just because – it violates a moral rule or someone's rights, but rather is wrong intrinsically. It is possible to be contemptuous of this objection, and to believe that it is simply an appeal to preconception or moral habit, and that the objector is the moral counterpart of the man 'who does not know anything about art but knows what he likes'. That analogy, however, should give one pause. Sometimes one has a sense of the goodness or badness of a work of art without being able, at least immediately, to articulate the features one would want to point to in support of this judgement. Jonathan Bennett has made a good case for saying that there is a similar phenomenon in moral life.

Any reasonable person will take as a start, not an end, to reflection the sense that an action is intrinsically wrong. One may reasonably begin by inquiring into the roots of this sense. Does it simply mirror the moral indoctrination one received while young, or the current attitudes of one's social class or caste? Is it instead (or also) connected with some deep and less parochial tendency to avoid producing suffering in others? The answers to questions like these should determine the weight one gives to one's moral first responses. If this is so, then we can arrive at the following generalisation: that an action endorsed by AC seems intrinsically wrong counts against AC only if the sense of intrinsic wrongness grows out of tendencies of thought that generally have good consequences. If seeing an action endorsed by AC as intrinsically wrong is strongly connected with tendencies of thought that are useful, then there are clear consequentialist grounds for considering it desirable that agents have strong inhibitions about performing actions like the one in question, and that (except perhaps in extreme cases) they not perform them. The non-consequentialist form of *O2c* however looks very implausible. If the tendencies of thought that lead someone to regard an action endorsed by AC as intrinsically wrong are not themselves useful, then it is hard to see why the sense of wrongness they yield cannot be dismissed as misleading and based on prejudice.

The preceding discussion of six likely objections to the simplest form of consequentialism, AC, points in two directions at once. On one hand, we can see that AC is indeed untenable. On the other hand, we can see also that some form of consequentialism is acceptable, in light of the fact that the objections to AC are plausible only if based on consequentialist considerations. Further, by incorporating the plausible objections to AC, along with points made earlier in the book, into a consequentialist theory, we are in a position to formulate an acceptable form of consequentialism.

Let us first get to the root of what is wrong with AC. It is tempting to place the blame merely on AC's simplicity, and to remark that in other realms of knowledge, such as physics, the search for simple unified theories has not been entirely useful. This, however, misses part of the point. Suppose that we were utility computers, without private affections or concern for our own interests, and were able to treat each case quickly on its own merits, without appealing to established rules or policies beyond the fundamental policy of bringing about what is best. Let us suppose also that all of those affected by our actions were also themselves utility computers, or had access to them, so that they could do a reasonable job of predicting our choices, and were not prey to insecurity and doubt as they contemplated a future shaped in part by us. Then arguably there would be no plausible objection to our governing our choices by AC. Thus the fundamental reason for the unacceptability of AC is that, in fact, we are human beings with human limitations. We need to allow for areas of spontaneity in our lives; we need to rely on others in ways that are satisfied by reliable personal commitments, and by a shared apparatus of moral rules and recognition of rights; we ourselves function by means of habits and mental sets, so that normally we cannot treat every moral decision as entirely separate from the moral decisions we are used to making. These are very general and familiar facts, but ethical theory must take account of them.

In taking account of them we can formulate an acceptable consequentialist ethics. Such an ethics will be framed, as it were, from the inside out, in that it will tell us not only how to make decisions, but also (very broadly) what kind of persons to be, and the former will depend on the latter. The theory can be referred to as 'attitude consequential-ism', in that the unit judged by the consequentialist standard will be most fundamentally a system of attitudes (and the policies expressing these), rather than the individual moral act or an inviolable moral rule; although it should be added that, according to the theory, individual acts sometimes will be able to be judged directly in terms of their consequences, and moral rules will be able to be judged in terms of the consequences of their general recognition.

There are three stages in the development of our theory. First we must determine when ethical reflection is appropriate at all. Secondly, we must determine when it is appropriate that ethical reflection go beyond appeal to relevant moral rules and rights. Thirdly, in assesing the cases in which it both is the case that ethical reflection is appro-priate, and that it should go beyond relevant moral rules and rights, we must decide what is an appropriate decision procedure.

The first stage must draw on our discussion of objection $O1a$. Spontaneity is a human value. Of course anyone is free to reflect on any decisions she or he wishes to reflect upon. But the danger to the normal pattern of human life, and to all possibilities of joy, is such that we must recommend that one normally not reflect ethically on choices that do not involve possibilities of serious harm or a major increase in well-being for anyone. Paradoxically, it has good consequences to have a policy of not, in most situations, thinking about consequences.

The second stage draws on our discussion of $O1b$, $O2a$, and $O2b$. If adherence to a moral rule, or recognition of a right, has in general good consequences, then it has good consequences to have a policy of simply following the rule or recognising the right in any case in which there are no extraordinary features that suggest that following the rule (or recognising the right) in this case would have markedly unfortunate consequences. The process of weighing consequences is one in which distortions, caused by selfishness or wishful thinking, can easily occur; and we are likely to make fewer and less ruinous moral mistakes if we are in the habit of following sound moral rules, and of recognising valid rights, in the normal run of cases. Thus, in the normal case in which a sound rule applies or a valid right holds, there is a strong conse-quentialist justification for not thinking about consequences.

The third stage of consequentialist theory construction is as follows. There are cases in which a perceptive and experienced person will notice extraordinary factors which suggest that, if a familiar rule is followed or a familiar right is not waived, great harm may occur or great good may be missed. The consequentialist justification for not thinking about consequences does not apply here. The point can be put in this way. None of us is infinitely flexible; and hence habit, inhibition, and mental sets play a major role in the moral life which justifies general policies of deference to moral rules and rights. But few of us are entirely inflexible; a decent person can from time to time examine a case on its merits, and can retain her or his decency while occasionally (for pressing reasons) deviating from a respected rule. In terms of human nature, we could say that, while act consequentialism would be workable only if we were all utility computers, rule consequentialism can be justified only if we are all martinets.

There also are cases, of course, in which the interests of many people are very much at stake, but it is not clear that any familiar moral rule or right is applicable or involved, or in which there is a collision of moral rules or of familiar rights. Because of these cases, also, there is a consequentialist justification for sometimes, in cases involving the interests of other people, thinking about consequences. Even when we examine consequences, however, we should not follow a policy which is simply equivalent to AC. There are two adjustments that we should make which constitute a deviation from AC.

First, we have to bear in mind that the risks of error are usually greatest on the side of deviation from established rules and from recognition of rights. Aristotle, in his discussion of the mean, recommends aiming to that side of the mean which is contrary to one's natural inclination: the naturally stingy man should aim, if anything, to be slightly over generous. In much this spirit we can say that a policy of being slightly conservative about sound moral rules and valid rights should, in the long run, have the best consequences, given the fact that our normal tendency is to be over-eager to find exceptions and drastic departures. In a case in which we think that breaking a promise will have consequences very slightly better than those of keeping the promise, this slightly conservative policy would have us keep the promise: in the individual case this might after all have slightly inferior consequences, but the policy in the long run will have the best consequences. In other words: to be a person who is cautious about breaking sound moral rules and about waiving valid rights has good consequences. Such a person, of course, need not be a rigorist. In a case in which it is clear that breaking a promise will have considerably better consequences (everyone's interests considered) than keeping it will, a slightly conservative policy is consistent with breaking the promise.

Secondly, in many cases in which we must weigh the consequences of actions that affect the interests of other people, we should substitute those people's value judgements of what their interests are for our own. If it is in X's interests that A occur, but X prefers it that B occur, then (all other things equal) in most cases we should bring about B. This falls under the policy, mentioned in Chapter 6, of, in a wide range of cases, acting *as if* the satisfaction of preferences of equal intensity is of equal value. This policy (along with the attitude it expresses) follows from respect for persons.

Respect for persons requires that we generally not treat other people as if they were manipulable objects or small children, that in our actions that affect them we seriously consider their wishes instead of managing their lives for them. Such an attitude has important good consequences. First, it protects against the risk that in managing someone's life one might be simply insensitive or wrong-headed, and thereby mistake a person's true interests. But, more important, respect for persons promotes self-respect and a sense of autonomy in others; it also promotes mutual trust, and a sense of harmony with the people one's actions affect. These are such important benefits that there is a strong consequentialist justification for a generalised attitude of respect for persons even if, in individual cases, the over-all consequences of doing what one knows to be in X's interests are better than the over-all consequences of bringing about what X wants.

If, of course, the over-all consequences of doing what one knows to be in X's interests are very considerably better than the over-all consequences of bringing about what X wants, even taking into account side-effects involving promotion and undermining of mutual trust, etc., then this is another matter. Respect for persons is commonly held to have limits. We do not always respect X's wish to take drugs, or for self-mutilation or suicide. Nor does a generalised attitude of respect for persons require that we generally respect X's preferences if X is a small child or is mentally incapacitated. Even here, though, our policy cannot simply be AC. Suppose that we are making decisions that deeply affect the life of a small child of ours. We will be concerned to maximise good consequences for that child, by, say, increasing the likelihood of the child's growing up to have affectionate relationships, a strong sense of autonomy, challenging creative activity, peace of mind, and experiences that might play a major role in a 'contemplative life'. But respect for the person that the child is growing up to be also dictates that we anticipate, and leave considerable room for, the child's making her or his own choices later; and this should play a far greater role in our decisions than it would if we were making decisions for our own life only. An analogous point applies to cases in which we are making decisions for those who are mentally incapacitated.

One other qualification of the attitude of respect for persons should be mentioned. Broadly speaking, we can distinguish two kinds of cases in which our actions affect other people's interests. First there is the case in which it is in X's interests to have A, but X prefers B, and our decision determines whether X has B at all. Secondly, there is the case in which X prefers B and will enjoy it whatever we do; our decision merely concerns X's ease of access to B, or whether X enjoys a great deal of B as opposed to a moderate amount. It seems to me that respect for persons does not require that we defer to other people's value judgements in the latter kind of case, as it does in the former. Thus librarians are justified in weighting their acquisitions in the direction of what they think good literature, as long as they stock some popular novels; and there should be no need for them to stock comic books at all. Government support of the arts can be tilted towards medieval music and can neglect pop music. However, if a small number of people think highly of a kind of music that requires government arts support to be heard at all, even if the people who determine allocation of arts support think little of the music and of the experiences it provides, respect for persons dictates that they channel some arts support to that music. We can make a rough general distinction between, on one hand, frustrating people's preferences and, on the other hand, deciding not to indulge them as much as they would like. Respect for persons dictates (with qualifications of the sort already mentioned) that we avoid the former, but not that we avoid the latter.

It finally might be asked whether, on the consequentialist theory being put forward, there are any cases in which one straightforwardly and simply should do what really has the best consequences. We have discussed adjustments to and deviations from AC that follow from the usefulness of respect for persons and of respect for established moral rules and rights. Is it ever right to apply AC in its pure form?

The answer is that we should follow AC in decisions in which the major direct consequences fall upon ourselves only. I am assuming here a view of morality and of rights that is consonant with Mill's *On Liberty*: namely that a person's treatment of himself or herself does not fall within the realm of morality, and hence cannot involve the violation of rights or of sound moral rules. If I am deciding what to do with my life, and the interests of no one else are greatly involved, then no adjustments are required by respect for sound moral rules, or rights, or by respect for persons.

Deciding what has the best consequences for oneself can, in some cases, require a sophisticated sense of the likely shape of one's life. If the choice is between starvation and having enough to eat, or between having a good education and having one so poor that one's variety of future enjoyments will be severely limited, then the decision is easy and very little knowledge is required. But decisions involving a choice of career, or marriage and other personal commitments, frequently are not easy, and cannot be intelligently made without a shrewd assessment of one's likely future.

Furthermore, if the value of a life can be more or less than the sum of the values of its moments, then there may be special difficulties. This is a point brought out by A.W. Price, in an interesting article on 'Aristotle's Ethical Holism'. Price contends that 'the totality of a man's activities and experiences through life is not a surveyable totality'. It must be conceded that we can never know as much as we might like about the shape of our lives. I shall argue in the next chapter that there are a great many cases in which the difficulties of judgement are so great that the only sound estimate is that one does not really know what is best, and many decisions involving the direction of one's own life must be included in this. But there is also a special tentativeness in value judgements concerning a life. For comparison the reader might recall the experience of listening to a piece of music, or watching a play. One easily may make value judgements of the music or the play, or of the experiences these provide, as the music or the play goes along. One can even think, after watching the first two acts of a play, that it is better than the last play one saw. But what happens in the remaining acts can drastically change not only one's assessment of the play but even one's assessment of the first two acts. The holism I endorsed in Chapter 6 implies that value judgements of a life should have this tentative quality. But the tentativeness, and its ramifications, should not be overstated. No imaginable developments in my life can much affect the value of the time spent in looking at art treasures in Italy, or can make it true that the time would have been better spent memorising the complete works of H.G. Wells. Even if we do not know as much as we might like about the shape of our lives, we know enough to judge with confidence, in many cases, which of our alternatives will have the best personal consequences.

One final point should be made. To be a person who reflects ethically when it is appropriate (and by and large only on such occasions), who in the normal run of cases cheerfully and naturally follows sound moral rules and respects valid rights, who is slightly conservative about violating these rules and rights even in unusual cases, and who expresses a due respect for persons in weighing consequences for others, is useful; but it should also be (to borrow Hume's language) agreeable. The intrinsic value of being such a person, rather than someone who makes good choices grudgingly or is not morally reliable, is itself an important datum of ethics.

NOTES AND REFERENCES

Much of the first part of this chapter is derived from my 'A case for consequentialism' (*American Philosophical Quarterly*, 1981). I am grateful to Professor Nicholas Rescher, editor of *American Philosophical Quarterly*, for permitting use of this material. Rawls's joke about Jeremy Bentham is to be found in his 'Two concepts of rules' (*Philosophical Review*, 1955), p. 27n. Smart's defence of spontaneity is in 'Benevolence is an overriding attitude' (*Australasian Journal of Philosophy*, 1977). The example of the choice between 1,000 units of good and 1,001 units of good (obtainable by breaking a promise) is from Sir David Ross, *The Right and the Good* (Oxford, 1930), pp. 38–9. Jonathan Glover's point about conflicts between innocent pleasures and the relief of suffering is to be found in *Causing Death and Saving Lives*, pp. 92–112, 292–3. The reference to Joel Feinberg's analysis of rights is to 'The nature and value of rights', in David Lyons (ed.), *Rights* (Belmont, California, 1979). See especially pp. 84, 80, 87. A good essay on rights whose approach is similar to mine is D.W. Haslett, 'The general theory of rights' (*Social*

Theory and Practice, 1980). Mill's claim that certain freedoms cannot be justified among 'barbarians' is to be found in the tenth paragraph of the Introductory Chapter of *On Liberty*. Jonathan Bennett's discussion of feelings as counterweights to moral dogma is in 'The conscience of Huck Finn' (*Philosophy*, 1974). Aristotle recommends aiming for the other side of the mean from one's natural inclination in *Nicomachean Ethics* 1109b (Ostwald's translation, p. 50). The quote from A.W. Price's 'Aristotle's ethical holism' (*Mind*, 1980) is from p. 351.

Views somewhat similar to mine are discussed, but not espoused, by Robert Merrihew Adams in 'Motive Utilitarianism' (*Journal of Philosophy*, 1976). What Adams calls 'conscience utilitarianism' (p. 479) perhaps comes closest to my view.

AC is modelled on act utilitarianism, a theory held by Jeremy Bentham and often imputed also to John Stuart Mill. It is act utilitarianism minus the utilitarian value component. A good recent discussion of forms of utilitarianism is L.W. Sumner, 'The good and the right', in W. Cooper *et al.* (eds), *New Essays on John Stuart Mill and Utilitarianism* (*Canadian Journal of Philosophy*, Supp. Vol. V, 1979). Ironically, act utilitarianism has a pathological feature which also comes into Kantianism from Kant's slighting established character (instead of merely reason) as a source of moral judgement: namely the tendency to treat a person's moral choices as in general atomistically separate from one another, so that every time it is, as they say, 'a whole new ball game'. For an account of a way of thinking at the opposite extreme from this see Chapter 2 of Herbert Fingarette, *Confucius–The Secular as Sacred*, 'A way without a crossroads'.

Chapter 8

Second Pattern of Argument

Our argument for consequentialism thus far has been a defensive one: that the strongest objections to the simplest form are plausible only if they themselves are based on consequentialist considerations. The picture that emerges of a viable consequentialist theory is more complicated than the usual one. Instead of consequentialism being in general the direct test of the correctness of particular moral choices, it plays a foundational role in a multi-level ethics. Consequentialist considerations determine the policies, attitudes, and institutions that we should adopt, which in turn determine moral choice. Consequentialism underwrites respect for human dignity and respect for rights. Some particular decisions should be made on a direct consequentialist basis, but I have pointed out how limited the area is in which we should simply set out to do what has the best consequences.

In this chapter and the next positive arguments for this complicated consequentialism will be outlined. My claim is that it provides the foundation for morality in much the sense in which acceptable theories of physics and chemistry provide the foundation for everyday judgements about the physical world: it provides a scheme of interpretation that makes sense of everyday moral judgements, and also provides a way of deriving and testing such judgements. The focus in this chapter will be on the second half of this claim, and in the next chapter will be on the first half.

In the last chapter it was shown that consequentialism does not conflict with the area of moral common sense that appears least vulnerable and liable to change: that is, the part that enjoins us not to torture people we do not like, and that disposes us not even to consider murder or theft live options in any situation we are likely to encounter. It is relatively easy indeed to show that consequentialism underwrites this area of moral common sense: that it has very good consequences that people have such attitudes towards torture, murder, etc. Indeed it was a commonplace among the early ultilitarians that the core of conventional morality can be derived from consequentialism.

If the consequentialism under discussion is to make out its claim to be an acceptable ethical theory, and thus foundational to morality, it must meet a stronger requirement. Not only must the core of conventional morality be derivable from it, but also there must be areas of moral judgement in which it functions better than unsupplemented moral common sense or than any rival theory. Otherwise it might be subject to the accusation of being bland, or of being in reality no more than a restatement of moral common sense.

In Chapter 5 it was pointed out that the two areas in which moral common sense could be improved upon are the area of difficult cases, in which familiar moral rules do not clearly give an acceptable answer, and the area of generalisations that are vulnerable to, or would be developed as a result of, moral progress. It might be claimed for some theories, such as classical utilitarianism or Kant's theory, that they provide a precise and definitive way of solving problems in these areas, such that moderately intelligent people applying the theory could be expected to agree in their results. I have already suggested that neither Kant's theory nor classical utilitarianism, whatever their merits, could possibly meet this strong set of expectations, and that Kant for one knew this. Instead the most we can hope for is a theory that meets the weak set of expectations described in Chapter 5: a theory that provides criteria for which features of a case are morally relevant (that tells us what to look for), and that provides rough criteria for how relevant features of a case are to be weighed once they have been identified. My argument is that the version of consequentialism under discussion meets these requirements, and does so better than any alternative theory or than unaided moral common sense.

Someone who is heavily influenced by Kantian ethics is likely to insist that even difficult cases can be solved by means of rules. Perhaps a familiar rule will need to be modified or qualified, or some special effort of interpretation will be needed. Perhaps (in cases in which two or more familiar moral rules seem to conflict) one or more of the rules can be seen, if properly interpreted, not to apply to the case at hand. The failure of casuistry has been the failure of this approach. A simple way of seeing the position is in these terms. If an apparatus of moral rules could solve all moral problems, then there should not be genuinely difficult cases. The persistence of these cases, even after there has been ample time to develop and modify the apparatus of moral rules, points to the failure of the Kantian tradition. It also points to a gap in moral common sense.

This gap can be filled by systematic attention to consequences of actions. Two points should be emphasised so that this theoretical claim is not misunderstood. First, we earlier defined the 'consequences' of an action to include the action itself and events that are concomitant with it. In other words, 'consequences' include what is present as well as future, and thus a test based on consequences contains no inherent bias in favour of the future. Secondly, it is important in assessing consequences to bear in mind that actions, especially of a drastic sort, often have subtle consequences (for people's moods, mental sets, and attitudes, and for climates of opinion) which are at least as important as their obvious consequences. This is particularly true of actions that violate established moral generalisations. What looks at first like a good result may include an increased willingness on the part of an agent (or of others) to perform similar acts again when there is even less justification; it also may include increased suspicion or diminished social harmony. All of these things are easy to overlook, but they (and further results that flow from them) should be given proper weight in any assessment of consequences. In the great majority of cases in which people are inclined to say 'The end justifies the means', the end turns out, on close examination, to be subtly spoiled. It is for this reason (among others) that we should be highly inhibited about violating moral rules whose general worth has been established, and we should be unready to look for exceptions.

The great appeal of a consequentialist approach to a difficult case is this. The consequentialist determination has us look at the facts, instead of mouthing phrases in a legalistic attempt to make them fall into a clear pattern or instead of relying on moral shibboleths that seem to have their appropriateness in very different kinds of cases. There is something usefully down-to-earth and practical in looking at what actually happens or is likely to happen.

The assessment of consequences is based on a limited set of facts: what is past and what would be the case anyway are excluded from consideration. I argued in Chapter 6 that the only facts to which we are justified in giving weight are facts about psychological states. Thus qualities of actions, or abstract relations of fittingness between actions and situations, enter into assessment only if they are reflected in psychological states. Again, this can be seen as bringing moral discussion down to the specifics of the real world and away from abstractions. 'What difference does that make to anyone's state of mind?' should be a recurrent question.

Classical utilitarianism would have us narrow our view of the facts even further. It would have us simply look for satisfaction or its reverse: for pleasure and pain, or for satisfaction or frustration of preferences. But surely there is much that is relevant to the value of a state of mind besides whether it includes satisfaction or dissatisfaction. The argument of Chapter 6 contains a case for saying that some satisfactions are valueless. It also contains a case for saying that some satisfactions (for example those accompanying hard and painstaking creative work) can have value out of proportion to the intensity of satisfaction. This suggests that in evaluating consequences we should not look just for the presence or absence of satisfactions (or dissatisfaction), and that when we do assign value to satisfactions we should not simply weigh their intensity. In assigning value we have to look at the psychological content which is the object of satisfaction or dissatisfaction, and also at the psychological context of satisfaction or dissatisfaction.

The *reductio ad absurdum* of the classical utilitarian approach to value is the case we can imagine in which we can adopt public policies that would bring about a society like the one described in Aldous Huxley's *Brave New World*. In such a society it would appear that satisfaction is maximised and dissatisfaction minimised; yet almost all of us have a strong sense that important values are missing, and that such a society should not be created. This kind of case should make us keenly aware of the values of creativity, autonomy, and human dignity, which are not adequately recognised by any value theory that simply assigns positive weight to satisfaction and assigns equal weight to satisfactions of equal intensity.

In Chapter 7 I argued that respect for persons would lead us, in many cases, to respect other people's preferences, and thus to act as if satisfaction of preferences of equal intensity did have equal value. To give people what is good for them, rather than what they want, is in many contexts insufferably paternalistic. However, this respect for other people's preferences should have its limits. It is a useful general attitude towards competent adults, but needs to be modified in relationships with children. Furthermore, even in relationships with adults it would be harmful for it to extend to criminal preferences; and it need not extend to preferences for addictive drugs, suicide, or self-mutilation. It also need not extend with full weight when what is at stake are further satisfactions of a sort that are already available and have been enjoyed, or (as in the *Brave New World* case) when the possibilities of experience of valuable kinds might be foreclosed.

All of this adds up to a consequentialism that is both complicated and imprecise, but that is still useful in relation to difficult cases. Let us suppose that we are confronted with a case in which a useful moral rule clearly does apply but there are unusual circumstances such that it is possible that following the rule in this case might be unfortunate. A policy of caution at more than one stage is a useful one to follow. First, if there is in fact little to suggest that the consequences in this case will not be good, caution may dictate that one not even entertain the question of whether to violate the rule. It is generally useful that we be in the habit of following established moral rules of a useful sort, and that we strengthen these habits. A tendency to look for exceptions weakens rather than strengthens these habits. And it must be borne in mind that people tend too freely to see exceptions in their own favour (that is, in the direction of what they are inclined to do), and that it is easy to make such mistakes.

Let us suppose that there is much to suggest that following the rule in this case will be unfortunate. At this point the consequentialism under discussion parts company with rigorism: we should not automatically follow the rule. It becomes appropriate to weigh the consequences of the alternatives open to us. But caution is still in order. If it looks likely that the consequences of violating the rule are slightly better than the consequences of following it, we should follow the rule. This is because of the risk of error, which is especially great in judgements of this sort, and also the difficulty of adequately estimating effects on our own character and on the general climate of opinion. The best consequentialist policy for such cases is, as it were, to play safe. Such a policy is likely to have on the whole good consequences.

If, however, it is moderately clear that the consequences of violating the rule in the case at hand will be substantially better than those of following it, this is a different matter. In estimating consequences, however, we must bear in mind not only the importance of the subtle psychological effects of actions but also the usefulness of a general policy of respect for persons, which (within limits already discussed) may make us substitute for our own estimates other people's estimates of the values that will be produced for them.

The case is clear for saying that this approach to difficult cases has advantages both over classical utilitarianism (which takes too narrow a view of the values to be weighed) and Kantianism (which looks helpless once we have exhausted appeals to rules). But there may be considerable doubt in some readers' minds as to whether the theory is really usable. Is it merely the best of a bad lot? Is it usable enough to be better than moral common sense unsupplemented by any theory?

The doubt itself rests on a faulty assumption, one at the root of the strong (and unrealistic) set of expectations for ethical theory. The assumption is that only a precise theory, which contains virtually no latitude of interpretation, is usable. However, this is not the case. We can arrive at reasonable judgements that one set of consequences is better (or is substantially better) than another even if there is no precise measurement involved, and even if it is possible in some cases that people of moderate intelligence who accept our theory will arrive at different judgements. If keeping a promise (whose fulfilment clearly means little to the person to whom it was made) causes you to hurt someone's feelings very badly, or to fail to help someone who has urgently asked you for assistance, then almost everyone would agree that the consequences of breaking the promise will be substantially better that the consequences of keeping it. The consequences of a public policy that brings about deprivation and misery for tens of thousands of people, and increased well-being for hundreds of already well-off people, are substantially worse than the consequences of a policy that relieves the worst deprivations of tens of thousands at moderate expense to hundreds who will remain well off. We can, and we do, make reasonable judgements of consequences without the use of precise standards or systems of measurement. Such judgements reasonably should have a provisional quality, both because of the difficulties in estimating the remote consequences of actions and because of the considerations discussed in Chapter 6 regarding the values of parts and wholes. But in the general run of cases we reasonably assume that if the short-run consequences of A can be provisionally judged to be substantially better than the short-run consequences of B then any better based and less provisional judgement of the consequences of A and B is highly likely to favour A. And a sense that one's judgements could be wrong and in any case are only provisional should not prevent one from acting on them.

Once we are clear about this, we can see that the theory under discussion is in a rough and imprecise way usable, and that it performs better in relation to difficult cases than does moral common sense unsupplemented by ethical theory. Indeed the approach that intelligent people who are not wedded to any ethical theory take to difficult cases points in the direction of our theory. An intelligent person, confronted with a difficult case, will endeavour to be sensitive to the situations of those who will be affected by her or his actions. We need to know how likely it is that those around us will be hurt or scarred by things we might do, or conversely how encouraging or strengthening our actions are likely to be. Intelligent people also try to arrive at a sense of the likely effects of their actions on their own character, and at a sense of how others are likely to react to their actions and what effects these reactions in turn are likely to have. All of this is part of a thoughtful and responsible pretheoretical approach to difficult cases. Consequentialism provides a systematic articulation of this, and is superior to moral common sense at its most intelligent in the way in which what is systematic and articulate is superior to what is unsystematic and not clearly thought through. Even what some people see as a defect in consequentialism, that in many cases it would lead one to say 'I do not know what is right in this case', can be seen as a merit if one realises that in many difficult cases we indeed are in no position to be confident about what is right, and if one realises also the dangers of moral overconfidence.

The difficulties of predicting the consequences of any action, especially the remote consequences, contribute to the justification for 'playing safe' by following generally useful moral rules (except in cases in which there are strong indications that the consequences of not following a rule are highly likely to be substantially better than those of following the rule). But how do we determine whether a rule is generally useful? There is room for uncertainty here: a comprehensive determination of the consequences of a rule's generally being respected is as inaccessible as a comprehensive determination of the consequences to the end of time of an individual action. But here again we can make a provisional estimate with some confidence. Presumably, also, because respect for a rule has such widespread consequences, in which the fortunes of an individual or a small group of people do not loom large, the chances of an unpredictable event changing over-all consequences from good to bad or the reverse are even less in the case of respect for a rule than in the case of an individual action.

Thus we can be reasonably confident that, say, the moral rule against torture is a useful one. And there is a good deal to suggest that most of the established moral rules we recognise are useful, and that they may have evolved in part because of that. One can say this without believing that all established moral rules are useful, and without believing that there is no room for moral progress. There especially are grounds for thinking that there is a need for *new* moral rules: that certain kinds of treatment of animals, say, or certain forms of social and economic inequality, which have been thought of as morally indifferent or not within the purview of morality, should be considered morally intolerable.

An instructive example of the creation of new morality is the fact that at one time it was normal practice to imprison debtors: not only has the law changed, but also we have incorporated within moral common sense the view that such a practice is impermissible. Such a view had once not been a part of moral common sense. Furthermore, there was nothing inconsistent or self-contradictory in exacting the penalty of imprisonment from those who could not pay their debts, so that there could be no room in Kantian theory for criticism of this practice. The only grounds for criticism, indeed, were that the misery created far outweighed any possible benefits. These are consequentialist grounds.

The general point here is that moral common sense is always vulnerable to criticism, that theory is required for this task, and that consequentialism – which asks us to look at how practices and requirements actually work – is effective in this. If it is part of moral common sense that X is required (or forbidden), but it turns out to be the case that doing (or eschewing) X creates misery and other sorts of bad consequences which outweigh any good consequences, then how can moral common sense's view of X be justified? We sneer at the taboos and superstitions of other peoples; should not X be put in the same category?

The claim about the opposing strengths of our theory and of unsupplemented moral common sense in relation to moral generalisations that are in question should be clarified. I am not suggesting that the theory will solve all problems in a clear and univocal way to everyone's satisfaction or that moral common sense is always helpless. Rather the claim is this. Moral common sense, which relies heavily on generalisations, is in a weak position when a generalisation is being seriously considered for acceptance or rejection. It tends to look for other generalisations to solve the problem, so that the resulting debate has an especially abstract and legalistic character. Much of the current debate about capital punishment and about abortion is like this. Consequentialism brings more resources, centred on a systematic requirement to look at facts. Recent consequentialist applied ethics, including most notably Jonathan Glover's fine *Causing Death and Saving Lives*, illustrates this.

It is of course extremely difficult to be entirely confident about what would be the consequences (especially the subtle consequences) of general respect for a new or strongly debated moral generalisation. Thus it would be entirely possible for two intelligent people who accepted the consequentialism under discussion yet to disagree about, say, the moral acceptability of capital punishment. We must continue to remind ourselves that only the weak set of expectations for ethical theory can be satisfied, and that there is no point in harbouring unrealistic expectations. The point remains that someone who puts the morality of capital punishment to a consequentialist test is in a much better position to arrive at a reasonable and probably correct moral judgement than someone who merely mouths generalisations, either about 'the sanctity of life' or about 'the fittingness of extreme punishment for extreme crimes'. If it were to turn out to be the case that respecting the sanctity of the murderer's life indirectly led (by weakening the deterrent effect of punishment) on the average to ten additional murders of innocent people, then should not respect for life lead us to protect potential murder victims by executing murderers? If it turns out that capital punishment is no deterrent, and that its consequences are on the whole bad, then is not speaking of the 'fittingness of extreme punishment' just an irrational survival of the primitive impulse to hit back hard? Whatever the facts are about the consequences of generally endorsing or rejecting capital punishment, surely we should judge on the basis of the facts.

One further point should be made. In the cases of capital punishment and abortion, there are a limited number of obvious options to choose among in deciding a general moral policy. We could decide, for example, that it is never morally acceptable to execute criminals, or that only those who kill policemen during the commission of a crime should be executed, or only those who murder for hire, etc. Some problems concerning moral generalisations, however, become even more difficult because it is much less clear what the options are. A good example is the problem of our obligations to the desperately poor of other countries. There is a very strong case, as Glover and Peter Singer among others have made clear, for saying that the present disposition of moral common sense (which regards anything we do for the desperately poor of other lands as supererogatory) on this matter is inadequate. But it is easier to see this than to create the new morality that would best fill in this gap. Part of the problem is this. It looks as if, no matter what we have already done for the desperately poor of other lands, anything further that we do (short of maiming or starving ourselves) will have good consequences. But this creates what Loren Lomasky has called a 'moral black hole'. The more we do the more guilty and inadequate we may feel, and in addition we may come to feel resentful and envious of those who do less. A saint can sustain effort in the face of these psychological risks, but most of us cannot. It is worth bearing in mind that morality exists primarily for those of us who are not saints, to present a limited set of demands that we can meet in a way that sets us otherwise free for private pursuits. The need in this case, then, is to formulate the right set of limited demands – not so great that it would be unrealistic to hope that most people would meet them, but doing the maximum good among the sets that would meet this requirement. Peter Singer's suggestion of something like traditional tithing may not be optimal, but it is a useful step in the search for a solution. No one should underestimate the difficulties, both in creating new morality where there has not been a specific moral requirement before and in the process of transforming a suggestion into a recognised social requirement.

NOTES AND REFERENCES

A fuller argument for the effectiveness of consequentialism in relation to difficult cases and moral progress would require detailed applications of the theory to specific moral problems. This would take much more space than this chapter provides. Fortunately others, with views on ethical theory at least somewhat similar to mine, have supplied such applications. I especially recommend Johnathan Glover's instructive *Causing Death and Saving Lives* (Harmondsworth, 1977) and L. W. Sumner's *Abortion and Moral Theory* (Princeton, 1981). Peter Singer's *Practical Ethics* (Cambridge, 1979) is another useful and provocative book. The suggestion about tithing is on p. 181, at the conclusion of an excellent discussion of world poverty. Loren Lomasky used the phrase 'moral black holes' in an unpublished paper, 'A refutation of utilitarianism', giving the examples of aged parents and Cambodia.

Chapter 9

Third Pattern of Argument

In order to see how the consequentialism under discussion functions in interpreting everyday moral judgements, we must see how close it is to being a truism, and how the gap between it and a truism can be accounted for.

Let us begin with the following truism.

Claim A   It is best that things happen for the best.

This can be seen as a truism if it is understood as referring to the outcome of a situation in which there are two or more possible outcomes. If possible outcome X is better than outcome Y, then it is better that X happen than that Y happen. Note that this does not say that we should do what produces X in preference to what produces Y, or even that we should be happy if X happens instead of Y. Thus the claim made is minimal to the point of nullity, and it is hard to see how anyone of any ethical persuasion could dispute it.

A near-equivalent to Claim A is

Claim B   It is best that things happen that have the best consequences.

I assume, as elsewhere, that the word 'consequences' is not to import a temporal bias in favour of the future over the present. Anything that is true of the world simultaneously with an event's taking place, but that would not have been true had the event not occurred, will be included among the 'consequences' of the event. Claim B can be seen as a near-equivalent to A, and as a near-truism, if in considering it we hold back from making certain assumptions about consequences. (1) We are not to assume that weight can be given only to psychological consequences assignable to persons or groups of persons (such as present or future willing, feelings, moods, etc.). Thus we may give weight to such things as moral stains, which can be properties of situations as well as of individuals and groups. This means that we are not to beg the question against those moralists who believe that certain actions create a worse world simply because of a moral stain, regardless of the psychological manifestations of this moral stain. (2) We should not assume that it is impossible for one isolable consequence in effect to have infinite weight, automatically outweighing all other possible consequences. This means that we are (again) not to beg the question raised by moralists who believe that some features of an event can be not merely more important than others, but can in some sense override the others or warrant disregarding them.

With this openness in mind, we can see that Claim B is very difficult to disagree with. Neither Kant nor any other anti-consequentialist philosopher is in a clear position to reject it. It would be, after all, open to such a philosopher to maintain that any event that includes a deplorable deed also includes something (a bad will, or a moral stain) sufficient for us to judge that the world is a worse place for the deed's being performed. Thus B is a near-truism. It could be rejected only by someone willing to say that the world is better for certain things having happened, even though it would be better that those things not have happened; and there is at least an appearance of paradox in such a statement.

Thus B is very different from statement AC, which was discussed in Chapter 7.

> AC One should always perform actions that have the best con-
>   sequences.

AC is, as we already have seen, very far from being a truism. It is not that we are now talking about 'actions' rather then 'events': after all, actions are events, and thus were included among what we were talking about in A and B. It is rather that AC has the clear form of a recommendation. It is possible to reject a recommendation as it applies to oneself, to refuse to make it to others, and even to decry it if others follow it anyway, while thinking the world better as a result of others following it. Something like this distinction was involved when Leibniz and others termed Adam's sin a *felix culpa*, a fortunate sin.

To ask 'Did it happen for the best?' is to ask for an evaluation of an event that itself involves a minimum of commitment. It is not even to ask 'Should we be glad?': someone might be saddened by Adam's sin while thinking the world a better place as a result. If an immoral action is performed that leads to a good deal of happiness, and to an upsurge of creativity and autonomy, it is possible to be so disturbed by the immorality as to refuse to be glad about this world; but someone who responds in this way (as one imagines Kant personally would have) can then insist that the resultant world is not a better world. A second alternative is the one that can be associated with Leibniz: to deplore the immorality but to consider the resultant world better than it otherwise would have been. A third alternative of course is to hold that nothing that results in a better world can truly be morally wrong. It is because the second alternative cannot be dismissed out of hand that

AC is not a truism, no matter how broadly we interpret the word 'consequences', and no matter how many of the assumptions normally made by consequentialists we refuse to make.

There are interesting differences, to be taken up in theodicy, between the choices made by God and human choices. Leibniz holds that God is a consequentialist: all of his choices are of what will have the best consequences. But this carries with it no encouragement for us to be consequentialists: even if Adam had foreseen the good consequences of his sin, and had altruistically committed it for the sake of these, it seems unlikely that Leibniz would have entirely excused him. Human beings in fact do not have God's knowledge of the consequences of events, but also a philosopher can maintain without inconsistency that they are subject to moral laws to which God is not subject. Other philosophers might prefer to put the point this way: human beings must form policies, and should make commitments of various sorts, and they must bear responsibility for their actions in the light of these policies and commitments. However the difference is put, there is a significant difference between an act of God and a human act. If (to take a case familiar in the literature) the life of one man stands between millions of people and happiness, we may be glad (or at least relieved) if he has a heart attack and appalled if someone kills him.

Human beings (to speak of what we know) have habits, mental sets, inhibitions, and acquired ways of structuring their visions of moral choices. A policy of trying, in every choice, directly to produce the best consequences denies any real hold to habits, mental sets, inhibitions, and acquired ways of structuring one's vision of moral choices, and thus is both inhuman and not humanly manageable, and thus is not to be recommended to human beings. This in broad outline is the case for saying not only that AC is not a truism but also that it is not acceptable. Let us explore in detail the gap between B and AC. This will also reveal the extent of the gap between B and our theory.

First, we can review the two assumptions which consequentialists generally make which we held back from making in presenting B. They were that in evaluating consequences weight can be given only to psychological consequences assignable to persons or groups of persons, and that no isolable consequence can have in effect infinite weight. My argument will be that both assumptions are reasonable and should be made. Their denial is not illogical, but it is preposterous.

In Chapter 6 it was shown that anyone who claims (as G.E. Moore did) that value can be assigned to something that is not a psychological state will find it impossible to answer the question 'How do you know that X has value?' There are only three alternative sources of any claim that X has value (or negative value). Either we know what it is like to be or to have X (because we have experienced, or can imagine, being or having X or something like it), or someone else knows what it is like to be or have X and we trust that person's value judgements, or we have a positive (or a negative) feeling about X. In the first two cases, what we find (or fail to find) value in is the psychological state of being or having X. Thus, if X is not a psychological state, and if the claim is that X itself, apart from the psychological state of being or having X, has value (or has negative value), only the third source is available. The third source of value judgements however is worthless. Our positive or negative feelings about X can generally be accounted for adequately as positive or negative feelings about the experience of being or having X, or of feeling the effects of X: they tell us nothing about the value of X apart from the experience of it or its effects.

With these general points in mind, let us look at claim MS.

> MS   When an immoral action is performed, a moral stain is a property of the situation which has – apart from the psychological states of individuals and groups that are involved – a negative value.

MS is not self-contradictory, but it is, when analysed carefully, highly implausible.

We must remind ourselves that the killings, torturings, etc., that we regard as paradigms of the immoral are in general actions whose consequences include psychological states to which we would assign negative value. Various forms of suffering can account for the negative value we immediately associate with such actions. In addition, a Kantian might say that the bad will involved in performing such an action has to be assigned negative value; and I already have indicated that I agree with this. All of this is sufficient to account for the feeling of something-not-good that a decent person immediately has in surveying a clearly immoral action. To assign negative value to a moral stain over and above the psychological states involved is thus unnecessary in justifying our feelings about immorality. There is no harm in talking about moral stains, as long as we are willing to spell out what we mean in terms of the psychological states involved. To refuse to do so is a little like speaking about magnetic fields but refusing to spell this out in terms of the behaviour of iron filings, etc.

Secondly, if someone wishes to speak of a moral stain, over and above the psychological states involved, as having negative value, we should ask how that person knows of this special negative value. The only answer can be in terms of a strong distaste for the immoral action in question. But a consequentialist can account for why one would, and should, have this strong distaste, without appealing to such entities as moral stains. If we as it were demythologise our moral responses, and see why they are as they are, we can recognise that misery and cramped and stultifying lives can account fully for the responses that lead people to talk about moral stains. To speak of the negative value of a moral stain over and above the negative values of psychological states then can be seen as a preposterous bit of axiological overkill.

To hold back from making the second assumption is equally unreasonable. We all agree that certain things (the loss of life, the denial of liberty) typically are far more important than others, and furthermore it can be argued that to be a person of integrity is to have certain things that one simply will not do. It may seem then that there are negative values associated with things one simply will not do which override all positive values, so that where they are present one simply need not look further at the case: in effect, these would be infinite negative values. However, it is important to bear in mind the distinction between a great negative value and an infinite one, and also between on one hand refusing in any foreseeable circumstance to entertain the thought of doing X and on the other hand deciding that in any imaginable circumstance X would be wrong. If the genuine and clear alternative were the destruction of all or almost all sentient life in the universe, some unthinkable things would become thinkable. If we bear in mind these distinctions, the temptation to assign infinite value to certain items, either for purposes of weighing consequences or for purposes of moral decision, diminishes considerably.

What could have infinite value? If a human life is to be assigned infinite value, then does the mathematics of infinity commit us to saying that a public policy that would save the lives of thousands of people who might die of malnutrition has consequences no better or worse than a public policy that instead would save the lives of a few people dying from a rare disease? (Any finite number multiplied by infinity will still equal infinity.) Or if a campaign to save the lives of the handful of people suffering from the rare disease itself costs no lives, but is so very expensive that a public financial burden causes millions to sink into miserable poverty, are its consequences infinitely good? (Infinity minus a finite number is still infinity.) If what is said to be infinitely good is a good will, and a bad will is said to be infinitely bad, then how do we reckon the consequences of an action that expresses a good will but indirectly corrupts others so that they come to have bad wills? Questions like these can have no reasonable answer as long as one clings to the idea that some isolable items can be assigned infinite value. Thus it appears highly reasonable to assume that this will not be the case.

We shall therefore read our two assumptions into all discussion of consequences. With this understood, we can formulate the goal of morality as follows.

The Goal of Morality – that events occur that have the best consequences.

This is, as we are interpreting it, virtually unexceptionable. Someone could reject it who refused to assume that in evaluating consequences weight be given only to psychological consequences assignable to persons or groups of persons, or who refused to assume that no isolable consequence could be given infinite weight. But these assumptions, as we have seen, while not tautological are highly reasonable. Someone could also reject our view on the ground that morality has specialised functions: even if in general we want the best world to be brought about, that is not the function of morality. But this seems highly implausible if one bears in mind that alternative moral codes exist and are always possible, and that a great deal may hang on which moral code is adopted. Morality is not the whole of life, but it includes some of the most important issues of life. Why should not a morality be fashioned so that it contributes to bringing about the best world possible? A philosopher who held a religiously based ethics could reject our statement of the goal of morality on the basis of the claim that morality can be understood as divine commands, rather than as a search for the good. But then such a philosopher would either have to admit that what God commands is always directed towards the best possible world, thus in effect accepting our goal, or alternatively would have to explain why God sometimes commands what is not for the best. Kant very probably would have rejected our statement of the goal of morality on the basis that morality can be understood as a rational system, governed by the categorical imperative, rather than as a goal-directed system. But then, as both Hegel and Hare have pointed out, more than one moral code can meet tests of the sort that Kant devises. Both a system that protects private property and one that deems it objectionable can meet them, as can both one that protects and one that forbids fox-hunting. In order to choose, we have to ask about the general worth of a practice or institution within which questions of rational consistency arise. Once we admit that more than one rationally consistent morality is possible, then it becomes difficult, again, to deny that contribution to the goodness in the world is a major relevant factor in assessment. Even if a morality must pass tests of rational consistency, it can have as its goal that events occur that have the best available consequences.

The whole of the argument in Part One supports our conclusion here. The morality we are familiar with can be seen most plausibly as a tool that puts pressure, in limited and manageable ways, on people to behave in ways that generally have good consequences. To be an effective tool, morality must meet certain requirements of interpersonal neutrality, and it must function in some ways like the law. But, finally, morality must be seen as a tool designed for certain purposes; and these purposes point toward greater goodness in the world.

If the goal of morality is that events occur that have the best consequences, there are two main alternatives in aiming towards that goal. One is always to aim directly for it. The other is to adopt an approach that is sometimes direct and sometimes indirect, but usually the latter. The argument of Chapter 7 shows, among other things, that the first alternative does not and cannot work. Always aiming directly for the general goodness of the world turns out to have such major drawbacks that it is counter-productive. Instead our approach must be usually indirect. This means that we promote the goal of morality best by having a morality whose broad character is like what we are familiar with: a morality that meets certain requirements of interpersonal neutrality, and that functions in some respects like the law.

Thus the gap between B and AC can be accounted for not only in terms of reasonable (but not tautologous) assumptions that would normally be read into AC but that we held back from reading into B, but also on the basis that AC represents a questionable (and in fact poor) strategy for achieving the goal toward which B (with additional assumptions) points. Most of the gap between B and our theory can be accounted for by the fact that the version of consequentialism put forward represents just one strategy (albeit the best) for achieving the goal of morality. To see this is to see how questions of general ends are both related to, and separate from, questions of how particular moral decisions should be made.

The argument that progresses from B to the denial of AC can be seen in more than one light. On one hand it amounts to a general derivation of the right kind of consequentialist theory. The derivation begins from the truism that it is best that things happen for the best, and the near-truism that it is best that things happen that have the best consequences. It is then argued that it is highly reasonable, in weighing consequences, to assume that only psychological consequences assignable to persons or groups of persons are to be given weight, and that no isolable consequence should be given infinite weight. It is also reasonable, viewing morality as a major tool in the design of human life, for us to ascribe to morality the goal of bringing about the best consequences. This goal is not best pursued by continuous direct aim on it. Elementary and familiar facts about human beings, and about the design of human societies, are such that habits and policies must play a major role in moral life, and we need a morality that is in some respects law-like and that meets certain standards of interpersonal neutrality. If morality is a tool, it must be designed with the needs and abilities in mind of those who will use it.

The argument also can be seen as a way of connecting consequentialism (of the kind put forward) to common-sense morality so that the former can be seen as the foundation of the latter. If we can derive the general character of common-sense morality, which was discussed in

Part One, from the general goal of morality plus the character of human life in aiming for that goal, then this provides an interpretative perspective within which common-sense morality can be seen. Common-sense morality emerges as not just a given, about which we might wonder 'Why is it like this rather than like something else?', but as a tool whose general character can be accounted for in a rational and systematic way. Thus the consequentialism put forward not only squares with the core of everyday morality, and not only goes beyond it in handling difficult cases and in testing moral generalisations, but also functions as an interpretative device in making more sense of morality than otherwise would be possible.

This completes the argument, running through three chapters, that a consequentialism governing policies, attitudes, and institutions constitutes the foundation of morality. The argument has shown (1) that plausible objections to the simplest form of consequentialism in fact lead us to, and support, the form of consequentialism in question; (2) that it functions as a foundational theory should both in testing moral generalisations and in yielding moral judgements in difficult cases; and (3) that it functions as an interpretative device, making sense of ordinary morality. The third part of the argument is in some respects the most important. A successful ethical theory, like both a successful scientific theory and philosophy, should change our view of the pre-theoretical and pre-philosophical world, so that what had seemed to be brute given facts emerge as connected to other truths, and as intelligible in a way that robs them of the tincture of the accidental and the might-well-have-been-otherwise.

This interpretative function is especially important in ethics. For most of us, common-sense morality retains the character of taboos and of commands spoken by unseen voices. Even a consequentialist, returning from philosophical reflection to the urgent practical demands of everyday life, can feel morality in this way. But if this were the ultimate character of morality, if nothing more could be said to ground it, then this would invite scepticism. Indeed, because morality is usually presented in this way, there is increasing scepticism. 'Why these taboos and commands rather then some others?' it is asked. The dogmatism of a morality that lacks a foundation leads naturally to relativism or nihilism, views which usually are held in as un-philosophical and unreflective a spirit as the dogmatism they oppose.

The alternative to dogmatism and to antimoral unreflective scepticism is that morality has a foundation, and that we can explain rationally both the content of the taboos and commands of common-sense morality and its spirit. If there is no plausible rational way of rejecting the claim that the goal of morality is that events occur that have the best consequences, then there are criteria for judging moralities. Morality then must be viewed as both justifiable and criticisable, and not as arbitrary and accidental.

NOTES AND REFERENCES

Part of the argument of this chapter grew out of my 'Vulgar consequentialism' (*Mind*, 1980), and there is a little duplication of actual language. I am grateful to the editor of *Mind*, Professor D.W. Hamlyn, for permitting the latter. There has been a slight shift in point of view between the composition of the essay and of this chapter, which may be more a matter of choice of words than of substance. There are both important similarities and differences between ethical theories and scientific theories. Some of the differences concern the role of prediction in science; others concern the precision and other qualities of scientific theories that enable them by and large to satisfy what in this book I have called a 'strong set of expectations' for theory. I have contended that ethical theories can at best satisfy only a weak set of expectations. In 'Vulgar consequentialism' I wished to stress the differences, which many philosophers have tended to overlook; and to this end I suggested that one could not properly speak of there being ethical 'theories' at all. Here I am more concerned with similarities, and therefore do speak of 'ethical theories', while continuing to maintain that there are important differences between anything that might be called a 'theory' in ethics and scientific theories.

Leibniz discusses God's consequentialism and Adam's fortunate sin in his *Theodicy*, included in Philip P. Weiner (ed.), *Leibniz Selections* (New York, 1951). See especially p. 510. Hegel's attack on ethical formalism is contained in *Hegel's Philosophy of Right*, trans. T.M. Knox (Oxford, 1967), Section 135, pp. 89–90. See also W.H. Walsh, *Hegelian Ethics* (London, 1967), Chapter IV. Hare makes analogous points, in response to John Searle's purported derivation of 'ought' from 'is', in 'The Promising Game' (*Revue Internationale de Philosophie*, 1964).

Part Four
Humanising Ethics

The Gap between What Would Be for the Best and What We Should Do

The progression of the first three parts of this book has been from the intuitive and everyday to the theoretical, from the surface phenomena of common-sense morality to the foundation. In this final section we will rise to the surface again, by explaining some facets of our foundational theory as it is applied to everyday problems. This should serve three purposes. First, it will make clearer the distinctive character of the theory as one in which the general and abstract goal of maximising goodness is tempered by the nature of the humanity to which recommendations are addressed. Secondly, we will be continuing the interpretative work of the theory, begun in the previous chapter, by showing how both the nature and limits of morality make sense in the light of the human-ness which has to be built into our systems of moral recommendations. Thirdly, application of the theory can contribute to practical ethics, as we study the role of personal commitments and of self-interest in our lives, and as we reflect on the proper character of ethical education.

The furthest point from the surface of morality is the theoretical claim that the goal of morality is the maximising of goodness. We have already seen that continuous direct aim on this goal is not practicable. Thus AC, which dictates that we always directly aim to produce the best available consequences, cannot be maintained. We need the lower-level generalisations of everyday morality, the acceptable rules among which represent general policies that contribute to the goal of morality. These rules can be internalised as inhibitions whose presence in us also has generally good consequences. Our need for rules and the corresponding inhibitions does not mean, however, that we must always be governed by them. Extreme cases are conceivable in which, because it is clear that the over-all consequences of violating a generally acceptable rule will be substantially better than those of following it, we should overcome our inhibitions.

A less extreme case is one in which X, which is the sort of thing that generally has poor consequences, will have good consequences, but in which an ordinary intelligent human being can be in no position to be confident of this. Here we may have to balance our degree of confidence that X has good consequences against what will be gained if X has good consequences and what will be lost if X turns out to have poor consequences. I have argued that the best policy is to follow a generally useful moral rule unless we are in a position to be highly confident that doing X will have substantially better consequences than not doing X. The policy is recommended on consequentialist grounds: generally following it will have good consequences. It is right to pursue this policy, and wrong not to.

This leaves two unanswered questions, though. (1) What if someone, because of superhuman powers or luck, believes that X will have good consequences, in a situation in which ordinary intelligent people are in no position to be confident of such a judgement, and is right? Should we condemn such a person's doing X? (2) If the goal of morality is that events occur that have the best consequences, does it not make sense to say that the truly right action in any case is the one that has the best consequences? We should urge people to perform actions that look likely to be right, but in the final determination the right action may be one that we reasonably would have condemned. Does not AC then, although inadequate as an account of how we should make moral decisions, give a correct account of rightness and wrongness?

These questions must be answered, but that does not mean that the answers need be either simple or clear-cut. On the other hand, I hope it will be apparent that any complexity or ambivalence that our theory manifests on these matters mirrors a complexity or ambivalence in moral common sense. There are some matters about which we are not sure what to say.

Part of the reason for this is that both moral common sense and our theory are designed primarily for cases that can realistically be expected to occur. Some of the cases to be discussed in this chapter are fantastical and most unlikely to occur. In their own right, therefore, they have no practical importance, but what we would say about them illumines the concepts we use in more ordinary cases. As extreme cases they serve as limits, or by being beyond the limits help to show where the limits are.

Let us begin with the first question, and suppose that a man brings about a cataclysm – something, say, that involves the deaths of a number of innocent people – because he believes (as it turns out, correctly) that on the whole in the long run this will have good consequences. We have two possibilities to examine. (1) The man who brings about the optimific cataclysm – let us call him Bloggs – holds the correct belief about the long-run consequences of his actions by luck. (2) Bloggs has access to an aid in prediction, say a cosmic computer, not available to the rest of us, or has a record of psychic power, such that we might reasonably be convinced that Bloggs's successful prediction of long-run consequences is not a matter of luck.

The first of these two cases is the easier. We commonly do speak of 'doing the right thing for the wrong reason'. We do not praise people who do the right thing for the wrong reason: they are at fault, even if matters turn out all right. As we shall see, later in the chapter, there are reasons why we would deny that Bloggs has done the right thing even if by luck his action brings over-all good consequences. Thus Bloggs is in an especially strong position to be condemned. At best, for reasons discussed in Chapter 4 in relation to 'moral luck' we will be less hard on Bloggs than we would be if his action had poor consequences; we also might be slightly less hard on him if he performed his action for the sake of good consequences than we would be if the action had been performed in a malicious spirit. Let us say that Bloggs throws a bomb that kills several people, intending by this terrorist outrage to produce a reaction that will avert a larger number of deaths and will lead to decades of peace and social harmony, and that Bloggs's deed somehow turns out to have this effect. We perhaps would not consider Bloggs to be as evil as the ordinary terrorist murderer, but all the same he is a dangerous fanatic. And by condemning Bloggs and his action roundly we discourage others from behaving as Bloggs did.

If Bloggs is able to convince us that he knows the future in a way in which the rest of us do not, the case becomes more difficult. We still have a good reason for condemning Bloggs and his action roundly, in that we want to discourage imitators who *think* that they know the future from producing cataclysms. Furthermore, our own allegiance to the moral point of view that forbids Bloggs's behaviour is at stake: if the allegiance is genuine, it is natural to express it by condemning Bloggs.

On the other hand it may seem unreasonable to condemn Bloggs for bringing about what he knows is the most favourable attainable balance of good over evil. Part of our dilemma could be put in this way. Morality as we know it is designed for human beings such as we all are. Someone who believes that God for reasons of his own has brought about the Lisbon earthquake or other cataclysms would be very rash indeed to apply moral judgement to God. This would be extending moral judgement beyond its proper domain. It generally is disastrous for human beings to 'play God' by producing cataclysms because of personal estimates of subtle or far-off consequences. But in the fantastic case in which someone actually knows the consequences of a cataclysm it may seem that our categories of moral judgement are out of place almost in the way in which they are out of place in respect to God. Further, how can we condemn someone who conscientiously brings about what is best?

Thus there are good reasons both for and against condemning a conscientious Bloggs who knows the future. If Bloggs is able to share his knowledge with us in a reliable and systematic way, then of course we all are in a morally different position. How different the moral position might become is difficult to say. One of the severe drawbacks of following a policy of AC is what it would do to the agent: such a person would be highly calculating, unspontaneous, lack normal human loyalties, etc. These drawbacks might be lessened if, say, Bloggs's cosmic computer, with no effort or calculation on our part, told us the consequences of our actions; but they surely would not be eliminated, and it seems likely that on many matters the cosmic computer would advise us not to consult it. Other severe drawbacks of following a policy of AC concern one's relationships to other people who could no longer view one as reliable in the normal ways or as committed to them in the ways in which we normally become committed to other people. Again, these drawbacks might be lessened if everyone has access to the cosmic computer and if its role becomes generally understood. Human life and human relationships might well change in fundamental ways. Clearly there would be, and should be, a change in morality if ordinary intelligent people come to be in a position to know the consequences of their actions. The change might not be as drastic as the acceptability of AC would be, however, if AC continues to conflict with spontaneity and if the personal relationships available to those seriously pursuing AC continue to seem less desirable than more traditional ones.

In the real world, of course, it is unusual for anyone to be in a position to be confident that an action that violates a generally useful moral rule will have consequences substantially better than following the rule would have; and in general to be in a position to be confident of such a thing is to have evidence that can be communicated and made available to other people in such a way that they are in a good position to arrive at the same conclusions. If I am in a good position to be confident that breaking my promise or stealing will, in the case at hand, have good consequences, then I can explain why to other people, with the reasonable expectation that many of them will be convinced of the distinctiveness of the case. To have a personal estimate, or an inspired guess, as to the consequences of my breaking my promise or stealing is not good enough. Any case that is visibly distinctive enough to justify stealing or breaking a promise carries with it (at least to a considerable degree) its own safeguards against imitation and the undermining of respect for moral generalisations. We can assent to the textbook case of the man who can save his sick wife's life only by stealing some overpriced medicine from an extortionate druggist without drastically undermining our inhibitions about stealing.

What do we say about the cases in which, as a matter of playing safe, we should not perform an action which, however, turns out to have the best available consequences? Was it in some sense the 'right' action all along?

The view that the right action all along is that which has the best consequences, even if we would be advised to follow policies that on occasion would dictate actions that will turn out not to have the best available consequences, has a certain appeal. It makes a central element of morality the doubt about what is really right that I have contended should be a prominent element in our thought about difficult cases and debatable generalisations. It might be held to be an expression of the near-truism that the goal of morality is that events occur that have the best available consequences. Nevertheless it misses an important aspect of the moral use of words such as 'right' and 'should'.

When we say that the morally right thing to do in a certain situation is X, or make a moral judgement that an agent should do X, we are recommending X in a way that normally carries with it more than minimal prescriptive weight. If we say, retrospectively, that the morally right thing to do was X, the word retains some of this prescriptive character even if what is under discussion is past and cannot be changed. To say that X was, after all, the morally right thing to do suggests at the least that, were the situation to recur, one should do X. In a case like the one in which Bloggs throws a bomb that turns out, in the long run, to save many more lives than it costs, and leads to decades of peace and social harmony, that is a dangerous suggestion.

What complicates the matter is that there is a retrospective sense of 'right', which operates primarily in relation to practical non-moral choices, in which what is 'right' is what turns out to work best. Someone who accidentally gives a poison victim the antidote to the poison, thinking it merely to be pain-killer, turns out to have done the right thing, as does the person who angrily strikes someone who (unbeknownst to anyone) is about to gasp and choke to death, thus dislodging the piece of food that has just blocked the breathing passages. The latter case is one in which someone behaves in a manner we would normally consider morally blameworthy, but we still are willing to say, 'Schwein in his rage did the right thing: it saved Bloggs's life.'

However, if someone asks 'Do you mean that it is right to go about striking people you are angry at?', we might reply, 'No: it is not morally right, not even in this case; all we meant is that in this case it worked.' The judgement that what Schwein did was in a sense (retrospectively) right is practical rather than moral. We might remind ourselves of the differences between moral and ordinary practical judgements. Both are prescriptive: both tell us what to do and what not to do. But the normal prescriptivity of moral judgements is more than minimal, and is conclusive: to say that something is morally right is to say that we should do it (or some alternative – if there is one – that is also morally right), full stop. To say that something is, or retrospectively turned out to be, the right (in a non-moral sense) thing to do is to recommend it, perhaps very lightly, only if there are no overriding reasons against it of the sort that would be taken account of in moral judgement. It seems to me that the prescriptivity of retrospective non-moral judgements that such-and-such was the right thing to do is very relaxed indeed. In the more serious context of moral judgement we cannot recommend striking a man with whom one is angry, when there is no reason to think it will accomplish any good, even in a case in which it turns out to have saved the man's life.

This is a point about the use of moral language, but it is also a point about the nature of morality. One can hold, as I do, that there is ethical knowledge, and that moral judgements are such that they can be well or poorly justified, without believing that moral judgements can be viewed simply as descriptive of some corresponding realm of moral truth. The nature of morality is more complicated than this, and the constraints on moral judgements include not only what we can experience of the value or lack of value of various states of affairs, but also the conditions that govern the workability of various kinds of moral recommendations. If to judge X to be morally right is a recommendation, and if it turns out to be an unreasonable recommendation, then this is an important constraint on our moral judgements concerning X.

Thus the answer to our question is that it is not reasonable to say that the truly right action in any case is the one that has the best consequences. The truly right action is the one we should recommend, should the case recur; and it often is the case that we should recommend a choice that may turn out not to have the best available consequences. Thus AC neither gives a correct account of moral rightness and wrongness nor gives an adequate account of how we should make moral decisions.

Some implications of this for the character of our theory should be spelled out. A standing issue for ethical theories concerns how, if at all, judgements of moral rightness, wrongness, or permissibility on one hand, and judgements of value on the other hand, are related by the theory. Many philosophers of the sort who are labelled 'intuitionist' have held that these are, in effect, two independent realms of judgement: that judgements of moral rightness cannot be derived from judgements of value or vice versa. Kant's position seems to have been this, although he clearly was far less interested in judgements of value than in moral rightness and wrongness. Writers in the consequentialist tradition are committed to producing a unified theory in which judgements of value are primary, and judgements of moral rightness and wrongness are derivative from these. An attractive justification for this is the one suggested by G.E. Moore in *Principia Ethica*: namely that 'right' simply means 'cause of a good result'. But, as we have seen, this cannot be maintained. Whatever assumptions about consequences we make or hold back from making, neither AC nor anything like it can be said to be true by definition. The issue against philosophers like Kant cannot be decided on the basis of the meanings of words.

The argument of this book is that the best available ethical theory is one in which judgements of value are primary, and judgements of moral rightness and wrongness are derivative from these. 'Morally right' and 'morally wrong' cannot be defined in terms of the value of consequences. But the constraints upon judgements of moral rightness and wrongness include the factor of consequences, and there is a strong case for saying that our experience of the workings of judgements of moral rightness and wrongness would lead us reasonably to favour a view in which they depend on judgements of consequences in the way contained in our theory. In short: judgements of value are primary, but a correct account of the relation between them and judgements of moral rightness, wrongness, and permissibility is synthetic rather than analytic.

One way of seeing the primacy of judgements of value is this. We commonly make, immediately and 'intuitively', judgements of value and judgements of rightness and wrongness. But, as the early utilitarians showed, the general content of our judgements of rightness and wrongness can be explained in terms of a systematic preference for consequences that we consider valuable. And if respect for a familiar moral rule has disastrous consequences this will be held against it. The argument of this book shows also that the form of common-sense morality can be explained along consequentialist lines. No one has been able to produce any remotely plausible explanation of the opposite kind, of judgements of value in terms of judgements of moral rightness and wrongness. Thus there is a strong case in support of a unified account of ethics, in which judgements of value and of moral rightness and wrongness are linked; and in the order of explanation judgements of value must come first. Our immediate experience, say, that interesting creative activity has high value, and that intense hunger and physical pain have negative value, cannot be explained in terms of underlying judgements of moral rightness and wrongness; but what would appear to be our immediate experience that killing innocent people and torture are morally intolerable can be explained along consequentialist lines. It should be added that, even though the judgement that X is more valuable than Y contains the prescriptive recommendation that, all things equal, X is to be preferred to Y, it is hard to see how this has any significant impact on the acceptability of the value judgement, especially when one bears in mind that value judgements do not have the social role of moral judgements and therefore can have much lighter prescriptivity. When one couples this with the theoretical grounds for regarding judgements of value as primary and moral judgements as secondary, it seems reasonable to regard judgements of value as (if properly made) resting on and testable by immediate experience, and to regard moral judgements as having a more complicated relation to immediate experience.

If the preceding is correct, and if the constraints on judgements of moral rightness, wrongness, and permissibility require attention to how well such judgements function as recommendations, then this explains why we must pay close attention to the character of the beings to whom the recommendations are to be addressed. It also helps to explain a fact which otherwise would seem bizarre: that sometimes it is wrong to judge that what one should do (that is, the action to be most highly recommended) is *the* morally right choice and is morally required. Besides the gap between what we should do and what is for the best there is a further gap between what is morally permissible and what we should do, and we cannot understand this without realising how the constraints on moral judgements include how well these judgements function as recommendations.

The simplest arrangement would be, in a case in which an ordinary intelligent person is in a position to see that it would be better to do X than any alternative, to say that X is morally required. But often the simplest arrangement does not work best. As we pointed out in Part One, it is counterproductive in matters which are too 'personal' or in which not much is at stake to subject choices to moral judgement at all. Moral judgement involves a heavy intrusiveness which has its costs, and sometimes the cost is greater than what is likely to be gained.

Even in matters that we do judge morally, we face the following problem. A morality, to be effective, must be viewed as something that ordinary people can live up to. If a sense develops that morality is a collection of impossible ideals, then people may well become more relaxed in their efforts to meet moral standards and in their attitudes toward others who fail to meet moral standards: such a morality cannot function effectively in promoting the social harmony, security, and other goals that morality is primarily designed to achieve. Thus any effective morality will have ample room for cases in which one choice may be marked as optimal but other choices will be regarded as morally permissible or as 'morally right' also. Saints and heroes will pursue the optimal alternative, but these actions are 'supererogatory': we cannot expect them of everyone. There are obvious examples of things that, in some sense, one should do but that are not morally required: giving a large percentage of one's money to the poor, or sacrificing one's life in order to save the lives of others. One further example might be adduced. A number of fantastic cases have been produced in the philosophical literature in which someone can save the lives of a number of innocent people by personally killing one innocent person. There is no point in discussing any of these cases in the detail they require: because of the horrendous psychological and social effects that taking an innocent life can have, it would be naive to suppose that a consequentialist would reach a decision simply by adding and subtracting numbers of lives to be gained or lost. But let us suppose that, in one such case, the circumstances are such that an intelligent conscientious person would reasonably conclude that to take the innocent life is the optimal alternative. For anyone who has the general attitudes and inhibitions of a decent person this would be very difficult to do: indeed it might be something that one could not bring oneself to do. For this reason, we might reasonably judge that it could not be morally required but was supererogatory. In an example of Alan Donagan's, a number of cave explorers will die unless the entrance to a cave is cleared, and the only way to do this is to explode a bomb which would kill one of their number. My sense (like Donagan's, but for different reasons) is that it would be morally right to explode the bomb. But we probably would not blame someone who refused to do it.

Any case of this sort, in which we cannot bring ourselves to do what is the optimal choice because of inhibitions vital to our moral life, is bound to be unusual. The more usual case is one in which we cannot bring ourselves to do what is optimal because it would disrupt the even flow of our lives, prevent us from gratifying ourselves in ways that we regard as normal, or disrupt our relations with those around us. Cases of this sort will be discussed in the next chapter.

NOTES AND REFERENCES

For a penetrating discussion of the moral and political ramifications of remembering, or forgetting, that we are human, see Camus's *The Rebel*. His novel *The Fall* takes up some of these themes in an interesting way.

G.E. Moore's claim that 'right' simply means 'cause of a good result' is to be found in *Principia Ethica*, pp. 146–7. He does not repeat this claim in his *Ethics* (London, 1955), but does say 'It seems to me to be self-evident that knowingly to do an action which would make the world, on the whole, really and truly worse than if we had acted differently, must always be wrong' (p. 112). In Chapter V of *Ethics* Moore defends the view that whether an action is right or wrong always depends on its actual consequences, rather than on its probable consequences. The suggestion, which Moore presumably would have found congenial, that act utilitarianism, on which AC is modelled, gives an account of moral rightness even if it is unsuitable for general decision-making, has been put forward by R. Eugene Bales in 'Act utilitarianism: account of right-making characteristics or decision-making procedure?' (*American Philosophical Quarterly*, 1971). For Donagan's discussion of the case of the cave explorers, see *The Theory of Morality*, pp. 177–9.

Chapter 11

The Role of Self-Interest and Personal Relations

The concluding point of the last chapter was that we cannot expect too much of human beings. If morality represents what we expect, then the demands of morality cannot be too great. Excessive demands are likely to provoke a reaction: by encouraging a sense of unworthiness they may produce greater laxness than we would otherwise encounter.

The classic Western response to this has been to recognise a gap between what is morally demanded and what we should do (that is, the action to be most highly recommended), applying to actions that fall in this space the label 'supererogatory'. It should be mentioned in passing that this is not the only possible response. One could develop two moralities: one (comparable to ours) designed for ordinary people who are willing to be decent and conscientious but not to make really strenuous demands on themselves, and a second designed for spiritually ambitious people who are willing to make really strenuous demands on themselves. This in effect has been the strategy of Buddhism. But only within a cohesive religious movement could an effective morality of this more demanding kind be formulated. Within a secular and pluralistic society the traditional Western strategy, of leaving a zone of the supererogatory, looks more likely to be useful.

Buddhist philosophy also contains a perceptive analysis of why we cannot expect too much of most human beings. The reason is attachments. Because people are attached to their pleasures, and to what they have learned to crave, they will not make the effort required to do what is best. Not all attachments are what we would normally term 'selfish'. People are attached to their families, and to those they love, and frequently care as deeply about the interests of those to whom they are attached as they do about their own. As a result they are inclined not only to place disproportionate weight on their own interests and gratifications, but also disproportionate weight on the interests and gratifications of those they love.

The Buddhist verdict on attachments is unqualifiedly negative. But it is too much to expect the ordinary person to try to lose his or her attachments. Such an attempt requires enormous effort over a long period of monitoring one's attitudes, and in practice it requires a special setting and special forms of discipline in order to be successful. In other words, a serious attempt to purify oneself of attachments is incompatible with anything like ordinary life. Someone who is seriously searching for spiritual perfection, however, will make the attempt; and such a person will be expected to behave in a strongly disinterested way. The more demanding of the two Buddhist codes of morality centres on the ideal of altruistic compassion, an attitude towards living things in which one plays no favourites.

This suggests two questions. First, how altruistic should we be? That is, to what degree should we come to give everyone's interests, including our own, equal weight? Secondly, how should morality be shaped and modified in the light of the answer to the first question?

The question of how altruistic we should be touches both on irtrinsic values and on consequences. We must ask whether, in general, it is intrinsically preferable to be an entirely altruistic person than to be someone who has some attachments and is prepared (at least in some contexts) to favour his or her own interests or the interests of loved ones. If the answer to the first question is negative, we must ask whether, for most of us, it is intrinsically preferable to be more altruistic than we are. We also must ask about the effects for others if entire or greater altruism is adopted by one person or by a group of people.

The question of intrinsic preferability is a nearly impossible one to answer. Clearly one can be in a really good position to assess the value of having the experiences and the states of mind of an entirely altruistic person only if one has been (and remains capable of being) such a person. But this in turn seems virtually inseparable from a commitment to entire altruism, and it is perhaps not surprising that the testimony of those who have experienced entire altruism assigns a high value to such states of mind. On the other hand, the testimony collected in the Buddhist literature is impressive. My own judgement, for what it is worth, is that some attachments contribute considerably to the richness of human life, and that what I can imaginatively reconstruct of the Buddhist ideal seems not quite as desirable as what I can imaginatively reconstruct of other ideals (such as the Aristotelian or Confucian) that do allow for attachments.

This very shaky and personal judgement is, however, compatible with the judgement that almost all of us would be likely to be better off if our attachments were fewer and weaker than they are: in other words that a shift in the direction of the Buddhist ideal would be beneficial to the character of people's experience even if the full ideal is not optimal. This is especially true with regard to our attachments to sources of personal gratification. As the Buddhists point out, what is gained in zest and excitement is paid for in frustration and in the boredom and restlessness that quickly follow getting what we wanted. There is an impressive case for saying that susceptibility to pleasure entails vulnerability to suffering. In later life the balance may tip towards suffering. To retain attachments but to make them (at least the selfish attachments) fewer and less intense is a moderate strategy which leaves room for some zest and excitement in life, but which leaves more room for peace of mind and less room for vulnerability to suffering. My judgement is that it is a good strategy for almost anyone.

What would be the effects of entire altruism? Human relations clearly have to change if one of the parties is as detached as Buddhism recommends, and something is likely to be lost and something is likely to be gained. What will be lost is a warmth and intensity which many people find very satisfying in close relationships; what will be gained is a cool relaxation which removes the clinging and possessiveness that normally attend close personal relationships, and which removes also the guilt which is almost inevitable if someone is not as much as is wanted in the life of another person. In some relationships, such as those between parents and children, it sometimes seems that the gains would outweigh the losses. This, however, is far from clear. Elizabeth Newson has argued persuasively that the personality development of children benefits from special concern on the part of their parents. Running through the Confucian literature, especially the *Doctrine of the Mean*, is the insistence that moderate attachments to others are enormously beneficial, and that lack of attachments is in fact inhuman. The Confucian case seems to me to be convincing.

In society at large, there also might be gains and losses resulting from entire altruism. There are obvious social gains if someone, or a group of people, behaves altruistically instead of in a grasping and selfish manner. On the other hand, it is not clear whether such cool detachment makes less likely the strenuous and demanding work required for, say, public health projects which benefit people in general: experience in Buddhist countries has been mixed in a way that suggests the importance of other cultural variables. (It has to be added also that, people who genuinely embody the Buddhist ideal are about as rare in Buddhist countries as people who genuinely embody the Christian ideal are in the West, so what one tends to see is the influence of the ideal rather than the ideal itself.) It may be that an almost neurotic intense concern for certain other people can stimulate such work more effectively than lack of attachments can. It also may be that selfish desires, especially those connected with personal vanity, are in many people closely linked to the sources of energy, so that entire accession to the Buddhist ideal would also lead to a loss of energy.

The picture becomes clearer if we ask what the likely effects would be if people in our society shift somewhat, but not entirely, in the direction of the Buddhist ideal, especially if the shift is mainly in relation to sources of personal gratification. Such a shift would not have a drastic effect on personal relations, except insofar as unselfish attitudes would improve these. The effects on society at large would be, I think, more good than bad. Perhaps there would be some occasions on which such a social shift would lead to a diminution of the energy available for worthy projects, but in a society with traditions of energetic work these effects should not be drastic. Moreover, they appear heavily outweighed by removal of some of the present unfortunate effects of selfish attachments and of excessive partiality towards family and friends.

Thus we can conclude, very broadly, that it would be both intrinsically worthwhile, and also would have on the whole good consequences, if almost all of us had fewer and weaker attachments, at least in relation to sources of personal gratification. Nevertheless, for reasons discussed in Chapter 1, we cannot morally require this of anyone. Morality must be concerned with conduct, and not with the state of one's soul *per se*; and furthermore there are good consequentialist reasons why most forms of selfish conduct, especially in personal relationships, are outside the boundaries of morality. We must continue to bear in mind the heavy intrusiveness of moral judgement. There is additional reason why we cannot require people to be more like good Buddhists. As we pointed out in Chapter 7, any useful moral strategy has to be workable over the long haul: it may be possible for short periods of time to get most people to exercise much more self-denial and generalised altruism, especially if there is some visible emergency to justify this, but in the longer run a reaction is liable to set in.

What morality can accomplish is this. It can circumscribe the area in which it is allowable to favour one's own interests or the interests of those one loves. Attachments can be allowed a large degree of free rein in, say, the disposition of money one has earned, and in decisions of how free time is to be spent, but not in decisions that involve breaking promises or taking people's property, or in the decisions made professionally by bankers, judges, doctors, hiring committees, etc. Indeed, a major effect of the development of professional codes of ethics, and of professionalism in general, has been the creation of realms of impersonal fairness in the midst of the competitiveness and favouritism of much of the rest of life. Any development that forbids favouring one's own interests or the interests of those one loves in a specific kind of case increases the operations of altruism without making unworkable demands on people to change their personalities, as long as there is a sizeable area of life left in which one can favour one's own interests and the interests of those one loves.

This suggests two points. One is that the interplay between morality on one hand and self-interest and personal relations on the other is hardly static. We can recognise important historical changes in the restrictions morality places on the play of self-interest and personal attachments. Changed attitudes towards nepotism are a good example. Another example may be changing attitudes toward conspicuous consumption. A hundred years ago virtually everyone would have thought that a wealthy person's wasteful and highly luxurious consumption in the midst of extreme poverty was without a doubt outside the realm of moral judgement; there is increasing doubt on this. Once again we must remember that the boundaries of morality have moved and will continue to move.

A second point is this. It is hard to discuss the subject of self-interest and personal relations without touching upon rights. A great many rights concern protection for those who are weak or vulnerable, and it clearly has very good consequences that recognition of such rights is incorporated into our morality along with very strong inhibitions about (at least in normal circumstances) even considering abrogating or violating the rights. There are, however, also rights claimed by those who are neither weak nor vulnerable; and many of these rights might be grouped together under the heading of the right to behave selfishly. Robert Nozick in particular has eloquently defended the right to behave selfishly.

What our discussion has tended to show is that it has good consequences that morality recognises some rights of this character; but this does not imply either that the rights recognised need be static, or that (any more than other rights) the rights should be respected in every imaginable circumstance. Also even if, in many circumstances, we do not and should not require morally that people behave unselfishly, there is of course the separate question of whether, nevertheless, they *should* behave unselfishly. Any morality that requires, say, that Bloggs give most of that part of his disposable income that lies above the poverty line to the poor would have on the whole poor consequences. But, delving into the supererogatory, we can yet ask, 'Should Bloggs give most of that part of his disposable income that lies above the poverty line to the poor?' This is to ask about the action that we would recommend to a Bloggs who is interested in making the optimal choice even if we would not blame him for acting otherwise. It is often said that some forms of aid to the poor discourage incentive on their part, but under anything like present conditions this cannot be said of all forms. For the purposes of argument we will assume that anything that Bloggs gives will be given intelligently.

There are some traditional bases for an affirmative answer to our question. The Buddhist ideal of altruism implies that the answer is 'Yes'. Jesus said to the rich young man (Matthew 19:22), 'If thou wilt be perfect, go and sell that thou hast and give to the poor . . .' (That this may be part of a systematic rejection of mundane attachments is indicated by Luke 14:26.) But let us agree that we are talking not about a generalised ideal, of what would be optimal for the very best human beings, but rather about what would be optimal for a specific individual, Bloggs. Further, we should keep in mind that we are talking not about moral requirements, let alone requirements at the core of morality (which, as we pointed out in Chapter 3, for consequentialist reasons should be the same for everyone), but about the broader question, which can lie outside of morality, of what Bloggs should do. So Bloggs's character and potentiality are highly relevant to the answer.

Two considerations seem especially important in framing our recommendation to Bloggs. First, unless Bloggs in fact has no major attachments to family and friends, we must be aware of possible effects of Bloggs's greatly increased altruism on these relationships. One option always is for Bloggs, like Buddha, to desert his family and friends; but this will almost certainly have its costs, and short of this the likely feelings of family and friends need to be considered. There is a risk, exemplified in Tolstoy's relations with his wife, that someone who is pursuing a saintly ideal will in the course of this inflict considerable damage on those close to him or her.

Secondly, any recommendation addressed to Bloggs must consider Bloggs's present psychology, how much he is likely to change, his limitations, and what he can sustain. Any policy of heightened altruism can be recommended to Bloggs only if it is one he can sustain, and is likely to sustain; it cannot be recommended if it would destroy him, or if he is likely to come to react strongly against it. As was pointed out in Chapter 8, any policy that requires of ourselves greater sacrifices than those about us are making will have psychological risks. This is especially true if, at the same time, we think that we might be doing more. If Bloggs gives most of his disposable income above the poverty line to the poor, but keeps some, there is a strong risk that, instead of feeling a glow of self-acceptance as a result, he will feel guilty and inadequate (for not doing more), while at the same time feeling a natural envy and resentment of those who are doing less (and who thus allow themselves more of the common gratifications). The net result of this could well be an increased sourness rather than sweetness of character, as well as the eventual abandonment of the altruistic demands he makes on himself.

Thus what we should recommend in such matters always must be hypothetical ('If thou wilt be perfect . . .'), and ideally the 'If' clause should include specifications of psychological strength, likely psychological reactions, likely effects on the network of personal relationships, etc. We might say to Bloggs, 'If you can give most of your disposable income above the poverty line to the poor without (a) damaging your closest personal relationships, (b) retaining an immoderate sense of what you should be doing which interferes with your self-acceptance and peace of mind, (c) coming to feel cheated of the common gratifications that you will be giving up, or envious of those who do not give up such gratifications, or (d) destroying the sources of energy in your life, then you should do so.' Even this hypothetical recommendation is very probably too general and schematic: there is a case for saying that there should be as many different recommendations of what should be done as there are people to whom they are to be addressed. We are far from the demands of morality here, and far from any territory in which generalisation is very useful.

Let me hazard, though, a generalisation that may be slightly useful. Perhaps, in the end (all things considered) very few of us should give most of our disposable income above the poverty line to the poor; but almost all of us should do more than we do. Very few of us are near the limits of our altruistic capacity. Any ethics can usefully promote greater altruism. The most prominent part of any ethics will be a morality, which sets forth what is to be required and what we will blame people for doing (or not doing). At the core will be requirements with regard to which we normally will not consider individual differences: they apply to everyone. But besides the goals of morality (the major ones of which are the elimination or lessening of certain crudely obvious kinds of harmful behaviour) an ethics can include in its goals the promotion of greater altruism. One way of doing this may be the formulation of ideals (as in the ethics associated with many major religions) of entire or greater altruism. Few can be expected to approximate to these ideals, but they may have a slight effect on the conduct of large numbers of people.

Finally it should be pointed out that one of the variables that determine the likely effects of Bloggs's greater altruism on his personal relationships and on his own psychology is the general social attitude towards, and expectations about, altruism. Greater altruism may be harder to sustain, and may have more undesirable side-effects, in a highly selfish society than in one in which altruistic ideals have considerable influence.

It would be easier for Bloggs to do more to help the poor, and more likely that he would sustain such activity, if there were a generally recognised social requirement to help the poor. Even if it is true that morality should not require entirely altruistic behaviour, there appears to be a strong consequentialist case for saying that here, as in other areas, more altruistic behaviour than is now common should be morally required. We could morally condemn affluent people who never help the poor, or who help the poor only very slightly, without requiring that they give most of their disposable income to the poor. Such a moral stance would still leave room for some selfishness and partiality: room which I have argued is needed and is important. There would still be a zone of the supererogatory in which some individuals, including perhaps Bloggs, should do more than what is commonly required.

The results of this chapter can be summed up as follows. The consequentialist theory that was defended in Part Three has implications not only in relation to the content of our moral judgement of difficult cases or of debatable moral generalisations, but also in relation to the form and boundaries that morality should have. The theory helps to explain why we do not morally require entirely altruistic, or even highly altruistic, behaviour. It also helps to explain the place of the supererogatory in ethical systems, and why ideals can have an important role alongside of morality in such systems. Finally, it helps to shed light on an area of ethics about which most of us have mixed feelings and confused ideas: the area in which self-interest and personal attachments may cause us to deviate from entirely altruistic behaviour. The argument of the chapter suggests, on one hand, that a recommendation of anything like entirely altruistic behaviour would be unrealistic for most people, and (if a serious attempt is made to follow it) would be probably harmful. It suggests, on the other hand, that almost all of us should behave more altruistically than we do, and that some moral requirement to this effect would be useful. Thus the theory both helps us in interpreting the form and limits of morality as we know it and also has revisionist implications.

NOTES AND REFERENCES

There are a number of good surveys of Buddhist philosophy: one that can be especially recommended is Edward Conze, *Buddhism* (Oxford, 1957). I have discussed the dual moral requirements to be found in early Buddhist thought in 'The Supra-Moral in Religious Ethics: The case of Buddhism', *Journal of Religious Ethics*, 1973. Elizabeth Newson's argument for partiality is contained in 'Unreasonable care: the establishment of selfhood', in G. Vesey (ed.), *Human Values* (Sussex, 1978). Nozick defends the right to behave selfishly in *Anarchy, State, and Utopia* (New York, 1974). A good standard biography of Tolstoy is Henri Troyat's *Tolstoy* (New York, 1967).

Chapter 12

Ethical Education

The thread that has run through much of this book, and especially the last two chapters, is that the precepts of morality as we know it are, and must be, designed for human beings. The recognition that morality is shaped by our imperfections and limitations is double-edged. On one hand it leads to an ethics more complicated and qualified than would be the ethics of saints with computer-like minds. On the other hand it suggests that, because good choice and virtuous behaviour do not come entirely naturally to us, an ethical life demands some degree of effort and preparation. If we were born perfect, with the essence of saints with computer-like minds, there would be no problem of ethical education. Because we are as we are, the problem of ethical education is an exceedingly important one.

It has been much more common in recent years to talk of 'moral education' than of 'ethical education', but I have resisted the former as chapter title for two reasons. First, our discussion has shown that important areas of life lie outside of morality. Most aspects of how one conducts personal relationships, or of how one designs one's life, lie outside of the range of moral judgement; yet they are important, and it seems desirable not only to educate people to make good moral choices but also to educate them to make good non-moral choices in these areas. An optimal education might lead someone not only to be morally virtuous but also to have personal relationships and experiences of a high order.

Secondly, Plato and other philosophers have made an impressive case for saying that judgements of value which most of us would consider to be non-moral play an important role in determining whether someone possesses what we could call genuine moral virtue or merely a conventional counterfeit. Let us grant that most people lead lives on the whole morally acceptable: they do not steal, commit murders, or cause harm to others in any of the other ways normally interdicted by morality. It also has to be said that, for most of us, in a reasonably decent society, a life that is on the whole morally acceptable represents the path of least resistance. Once one has been acculturated and has been given the right habits, it is usually easier to do what is expected than it is to break loose and risk hostility and punishment. This is not to say that behaving in a morally acceptable way is always easy, even in the best regulated society; but it is to claim that by and large, for most of us, behaviour that is on the whole morally acceptable represents a less difficult path than flagrantly immoral behaviour. (The materials to lead someone to behave on the whole in a morally acceptable way are simple and common; the ways in which becoming highly or dependably moral, and coming to behave morally even in difficult cases or in the face of great temptation, require more sophisticated education will be discussed later.) There is a case, accordingly, for saying that most people who are commonly judged to be highly immoral either have not been acculturated or given the right habits or are emotionally disturbed or so generally inept that they cannot successfully pursue the path that most of us find not all that difficult. In a chaotic or wicked society, such as that of Nazi Germany, this is no longer true; in such a society it may take much more effort and courage to behave in a morally virtuous way than not so to behave. In any society, also, there are cases of unusual temptation, in which to violate acceptable morality looks attractive and easy; here again moral virtue becomes difficult.

It may seem reasonable to attribute genuine moral virtue only to someone who would behave in a morally virtuous manner even when it was easy and tempting to behave otherwise. But then, if we consider extreme temptations, such as that represented by a ring of invisibility (which would guarantee that one could act in any way with impunity and without being known), it appears that few people possess genuine moral virtue. In Book II of Plato's *Republic*, Glaucon indeed suggests that no one would pass this test. 'Suppose now that there were two such magic rings, and the just put on one of them and the unjust the other; no man can be imagined to be of such an iron nature that he would stand fast in justice.' The Myth of Er in Book X of the *Republic* may be considered a reply to this challenge: some people, cast loose from the demands normally made on them, still will choose well. (It seems clear that Plato believed that Socrates, if given a ring of invisibility, would yet continue to behave justly.) It is remarked of a reincarnated soul who chooses a wicked and inferior life that he 'had dwelt in a well-ordered State, but his virtue was a matter of habit only, and he had no philosophy'.

Thus to be morally virtuous in a sense that implies dependability – so that one would behave virtuously even in a corrupt or wicked society or in a situation of great temptation – requires philosophy as well as habit. By 'philosophy' I think that Plato here means an intelligent set of values, and a clear understanding based on these values of why actions customarily judged to be morally wrong are indeed morally wrong. Common experience suggests that Plato is right in thinking that most people's habits of virtue would give way in the face of a temptation such as that represented by a ring of invisibility. Why would one not, if given such a ring, take the opportunity to steal or kill in order to acquire wealth, power, and the gratifications that these bring? There are only two possible reasons. One may have a clear and firm sense of why stealing and killing are wrong. The other reason is that one has a clear awareness that wealth and power, and the gratifications that these bring, are of far less value than are other things (which would be lost or impaired as a result of immoral action) such as psychological harmony. Someone like Socrates, who can combine both reasons, is proof against temptation.

Ethical education should have two components, in order to promote what Plato calls 'habit' and 'philosophy'. At its best, ethical education might lead to the emergence of a number of adults who approximate to Socrates at least in having intelligent values and a clear and firm sense of how conventional moral requirements make sense. In our society, though, it appears too much to expect that the great majority of adults will come to have these qualities. But it is important that as many as possible of other adults, and of adolescents, behave in a morally acceptable way. Therefore acculturation that includes the inculcation of habits of not stealing, breaking promises, harming others, etc., must be an important part of ethical education. Even for a Socrates this acculturation will be a necessary component of ethical education; for others, it may be very nearly the whole.

Let us call the two components of ethical education 'acculturation' and 'philosophical understanding'. As has already been indicated, a major part of acculturation will be the instilling of the right kinds of habits of behaviour. The importance of this should not be under-estimated. It is very easy to say, 'Of course people should understand *why* certain kinds of behaviour are wrong.' But this understanding becomes more possible when our habit and expectations have accustomed us to the idea that stealing, harming others, etc., indeed *are* wrong. Furthermore, we must bear in mind that any society needs to provide ethical education to virtually everybody; and that attitudes and behaviour of the wrong sort on the part of children and adolescents, and of people who are slow to understand justifications of morality, can represent a threat to members of society. We cannot wait for people to understand why they should behave in morally acceptable ways before we expect them to behave in these ways.

Traditionally, ethical education took place both in a child's home and in school, and this remains ideal. But in recent years there has been a growing feeling that the home is not always a reliable provider of ethical education. This poses special problems for the school, especially in a country like the United States in which religious instruction or bias is not allowed in a public (state-operated) school. It may seem that ethical instruction is a shadowy counterpart to religious instruction: it too takes sides in matters which may well be open to controversy. If the state should not inculcate religious beliefs, then (it will be contended) it should not inculcate values or moral views either. A solution may be to keep ethical education very general and vague, or constantly to indicate alternative points of view and let the student make up her or his mind, or not to have ethical education in state-operated schools at all.

All of these solutions seem to me to be extremely unsatisfactory. A society must ensure that its members have had an adequate ethical education. One that is general and vague is liable to seem like twaddle, and to be treated as such by discerning students. Further, we cannot treat matters like whether it is acceptable to steal or to harm others as open questions in the classroom. In the end, of course, every student will make up her or his mind about what is morally acceptable; but it may aid the process if we treat certain answers as obviously right (as indeed they are). Any student who chooses to believe that Columbus never sailed to the New World, or that two plus two equals five, cannot in the final reckoning be prevented from nourishing these beliefs; but this does not mean that a school should treat these as open questions.

In the end a school cannot treat the moral acceptability of stealing or of physically harming others as open matters for the simple reason that these kinds of behaviour cannot be tolerated within the school. Nor are they tolerated in society at large. This is pertinent to the worry about neutrality of values. Our society is emphatically not neutral about stealing or about causing harm to others. This suggests that a reasonable strategy in ethical education in the schools will begin by distinguishing between questions such as these which are not legitimately open to controversy and questions (such as those centring around abortion, euthanasia, and capital punishment) about which there is no embedded consensus vital to the running of society, and which therefore may be treated as controversial. Clearly judgements of the value of various kinds of experiences, and of ways of life, must by this standard be treated as controversial. A school can reasonably hope to inculcate habits and attitudes related to such matters as stealing and promise-keeping. With regard to such matters as abortion and euthanasia, or questions of what is most valuable in life, it can promote discussion of alternative points of view, and encourage students to arrive at intelligent judgements.

The first part of this recommendation may seem hopelessly old-fashioned. It amounts to a recommendation that moral rules, drawn from the core of morality, be taught in the classroom. Lawrence Kohlberg has rejected the teaching of moral rules as 'indoctrinative'. In this he has argued from an explicitly Platonic view that to learn virtue is to learn the unifying virtue of justice; knowledge of the good is not the same as correct opinion or acceptance of conventional beliefs. Therefore 'the teaching of virtue is the asking of questions and the pointing of the way, not the giving of answers'. There is also the more down-to-earth objection that the 'indoctrinative' approach, which used to be common, amounted to 'preaching and imposition of the rules and values of the teacher'.

Kohlberg's appeal to Plato is misconstrued. The Platonic view he cites concerns the advanced stages of ethical education. It is true, as we have seen, that Plato believed that ethical knowledge requires much more than mere acceptance of conventional moral generalisations and the possession of the right kinds of habits. Plato indeed believed that to learn virtue is to learn the unifying virtue of justice. But none of this is to deny that inculcation of the right habits plays a vital role in the initial stages of ethical education. Nor is it to deny that many people will not advance much beyond these initial stages. Kohlberg has appealed to Plato's view of the advanced stages and the optimal final result of ethical education as if it were an account of the whole of ethical education.

The down-to-earth objection that the 'indoctrinative' approach amounts to preaching and imposition of values must be taken more seriously. But first we must distinguish between a teacher's imposition of personal values, on one hand, and imposition of core societal moral judgements on the other. In most contexts it would be improper in a state-operated school for a teacher who has, say, strong views in favour of or against abortion to impose these views on the children in the classroom. But this surely is not to condemn imposition of the view that stealing or beating up those one dislikes is wrong. What I am suggesting is *not* that only views embedded in a society's core morality are correct, but merely that it is generally useful, in preserving a healthy relation between state-operated schools and the societies they serve, that it be understood that only views embedded in the society's core morality are to be indoctrinated. In unusual and urgent circumstances there may be exceptions to this: we think that teachers in Germany should have spoken out both before and after the Nazis came to power. But any teacher would be advised to be cautious in claiming an exception to this general rule of restraint. Any case of indoctrinating a correct but controversial moral view may set a dangerous precedent for cases of indoctrinating incorrect and controversial moral views: it is risky to set aside too lightly the neutrality of the state-operated school.

Even if a teacher attempts to indoctrinate students only with core societal moral judgements, if this is mishandled there is a danger that it may produce a reaction and be counterproductive. It would be naive for a teacher to think that merely articulating a moral claim is effective in getting students to believe it. Someone who wishes to inculcate core moral beliefs, dealing with matters such as stealing, breaking promises, and the like, would do well not to be too assertive about them. Bear in mind the fact that the teacher who has the quietest classroom is usually not the one who periodically shouts 'Students must be quiet' or who writes this on the blackboard. Along much the same lines it would be extremely naive to suppose that a teacher or a parent can inculcate moral rules by means of catechism, or by having students write them down. Indeed, this style of presentation is more like setting up a target, which invites violation, than it is like persuasion.

Probably the most effective way of first presenting the core societal moral judgements is to treat them like background noise contained in what one is saying or doing. Of course one does not steal or break promises; that goes without saying; and, if someone steals or breaks a promise, that might be occasion for surprise rather than anger. Anything which is obviously correct does not require a laboured propaganda effort to be taught, and laboured propaganda efforts justifiably provoke suspicion and doubt.

If the rules contained in the core of societal morality are discussed directly, they should not be treated as dicta, but rather more like theorems. A basis for them can be presented. There are two major lines of justification, which need not be viewed as competitive: they can both be entirely or largely correct. First there is the consequentialist justification argued for in this book. Acceptable morality represents strong social requirements that are such that general respect for them has much better consequences than would widespread disregard. At the core of morality are requirements that are vital for the security and well-being of members of society generally. Even a child can be got to see how nasty and unpleasant life would be if people very often stole from each other or beat up those they disliked.

A second line of justification owes more to the Kantian tradition, although I have argued that what is valid in it can be accommodated (and explained) within a consequentialist theory. The rules in the core of societal morality can be presented as more particular embodiments of a highly general principle, such as that of respect for persons. (Respect for persons itself has a strong consequentialist justification.) This can be reinforced by Hare's universalisability principle: if it is wrong for X (or anyone else) to steal from you, then what makes it all right for you to steal from X?

It cannot too heavily be stressed that, one way or another, the core of societal morality must be conveyed to children very early in their education. The risks which come from this not having taken place are frightful. And we must not be so preoccupied with what we hope will take place in the advanced stages of ethical education that we forget the initial stages.

The core of societal morality consists of rules (against promise-breaking, harming others, etc.), and what will be inculcated in the initial stages of ethical education will be these rules. At later stages it may be appropriate to point out that moral rules can have exceptions, and to discuss possible exceptions. But two cautions are in order. If this is done too early, children will be encouraged not to take moral rules seriously. It is important that all or almost all of us do take the rules at the core of morality seriously, that we internalise them, and that even as adults we have strong inhibitions about stealing, breaking our promises, killing, etc. Secondly, when exceptions are discussed, it is important to stress how rare they are. If moral dilemmas (such as the case of the man who can get medicine for his dying wife only by stealing it from an extortionate druggist) are presented, it is important that they be presented cautiously, and that the uncommon nature of the cases discussed be underlined.

What should advanced ethical education consist of? Two fashionable answers need to be dismissed. One is that ethical education should consist of 'values clarification': that is, the student should be encouraged to explore what she or he really believes in. This may be in part a reaction to the constraints on what can be taught in a state-operated school in a modern secular society. But the implication, that finally one can believe what one likes, and that one point of view is just as good as another, is not lost on students. Andrew Oldenquist has dealt very effectively in a review essay with the shallow relativism of the 'values clarification' school of moral education. Let me point out that even a teacher who is properly unwilling to impose his or her values on students can make it clear that ethical questions are serious ones, that there are cognitive standards governing the kinds of reasoning and evidence that one can produce in relation to them, and that there is no reason to think that all answers are equally valid. If a youthful proto-Hitler is in the classroom there is no excuse for saying 'Well, what you say is right for you', or 'I can see where you are coming from', or 'You must get in touch with your feelings and see what is right for you'.

The other fashionable answer consists of Lawrence Kohlberg's stages of moral development, in which a student is led to the highest stage of judgements on principle. Kohlberg's schematism owes a good deal to Kant, although a partial misreading of Kant is at work: a layer of moral rules intervening between the most general principles and particular cases plays a role in Kantian ethics which finds no close counterpart in Kohlberg's scheme. Be that as it may, our discussion in this book (especially in Chapters 2 through 5) suggests the weakness of treating moral education as leading to the ultimate goal of judgement on the basis of highly general principle.

The role of sensitivity in ethics is often neglected by those in the Kantian tradition. This is a symptom of a tendency to over-intellectualise ethical judgement, and to ignore the role of sympathy (discussed in Chapter 5). People who commit immoral actions may or may not be more stupid than the average person, but it does seem to be the case that they usually are insensitive to the feelings and the details of the consequent lives of their victims. It is not impossible to be sensitive to someone's feelings and experiences and to be sympathetic to the suffering these may include, and yet to behave immorally to that person; but it is difficult. Thus 'care and sensitivity to the needs of others', to borrow language from Carol Gilligan's study of the moral development of women, should be a major product of ethical education. Kohlberg's scheme encourages casuistry in the classroom. It is much more important to get students to have a sense of how people are affected by various kinds of immoral action, and to care about the experiences of victims.

Let me spell out this point. Care and sensitivity are important to moral choice in two ways. First, in a great many situations people who have been acculturated are very likely to do what is right unthinkingly, without the benefit of care and sensitivity: they will unreflectively and almost automatically choose, say, not to steal or to beat up people they dislike. But someone who has not been acculturated may be saved from performing a wrong action by sensitivity to, and some care about, the feelings and likely experiences of potential victims. Secondly, there are cases in which, because of unusual features or temptation, even an acculturated person can easily go wrong. Care and sensitivity can make a great difference in these cases.

Ethical education in the advanced stages should contain three components. First, there should be serious discussion of values. This is justified not only by the role that value judgements play in determining moral choice, but also by their role in a student's eventual choice of career and general style of life. Many people accept dull jobs because the salary is good, and over a long period of time come to feel constrained and thwarted; many people also embark on styles of life that provide great satisfactions in the short run but in the long run prove to be subtly unsatisfactory. These are not immoral decisions, but they are poor decisions; and ethical education should give people a chance not to make them. It is sometimes surprising that people who are in general intellectually sophisticated turn out to have been unsophisticated and thoughtless in their value systems, and this surely is a sign of inadequate ethical education.

If what has been said earlier in this book (chiefly in Chapter 6) about value judgements is correct, then serious discussion of values must take the form of getting students to see what it is like (especially in the long haul) to live according to various value judgements. Works of imaginative literature can be useful in this. Indeed there is a species of novel (Johnson's *Rasselas*, Voltaire's *Candide*, the novels of Sartre) that features thought experiments with systems of values. But also students must be encouraged to develop on their own a sense of what it would be like over the long run to pursue certain systems of value. That this is relevant to what we would consider moral judgement is made clear by Plato's discussion in *The Republic* of what it is like to be the tyrant. Untrammelled immorality may seem attractive until one inquires closely into the psychological details. One of the reasons why one should not want to be immoral consists in the destructive effect of immorality on psychological harmony and integrity, and it is useful to get students to see this.

A second component of advanced ethical education should be the promotion of sensitivity to others, and to the consequences of actions. Clearly this can contribute to creating and maintaining fulfilling personal relationships. But also, as already has been pointed out, immoral actions are usually perpetrated by people who are insensitive to the feelings and the consequent experiences of the victims. A developed sense of what it is like to be cheated, stolen from, or mistreated in some other way will promote the inclination to behave morally.

Sensitivity to consequences should not stop at the direct harm that an action may do to other people. Much of the harm produced by immoral actions consists of undermining of trust, and promotion of an increased sense of insecurity and of social disorder. A student should become sensitive not only to the feelings and experiences of direct victims of immorality, but also to what it is like to live in a situation in which one does not trust one's neighbours or companions, or in which the possibility of sudden violence or of mistreatment of some other sort seems real. In dealing with cases in which there may seem to be more justification for theft than there normally is, students should be led to get a sense of what it is like to be a shopkeeper or store manager who is constantly worried about items being stolen. A sense of the unpleasantness of being treated suspiciously by such a person is also relevant to deliberations about the consequences of acts of theft.

A third component of advanced ethical education should be discussion of moral rules and principles. At this point a student will have internalised rules from the core of accepted morality: it will be natural to discuss further what the justification for these is, and what exceptions there might be. Our earlier remarks indicate the importance of caution here. Once the idea that there are exceptions has been presented, a common response is to find exceptions more freely than is justified. This can be countered by careful attention to the subtle as well as the obvious consequences of actions, and also by proper emphasis on the risks of misjudgement.

Principles represent a separate subject of considerable interest. Ethical education must be education of character, and this is especially true at the advanced stages. It is important to get students to realise that in a wide variety of difficult cases quick and reliable calculation of consequences is impossible. Instead one must approach problems by means of the system of responses inherent in being a certain sort of person. To be a person of character is to have certain things that (in any normal situation, or situation remotely like a normal one) one simply does not do, and to have certain factors that one typically looks for in a morally problematic situation. These shibboleths and priorities can be expressed in the form of principles. It will have good consequences to have a good set of strong and clearly articulated principles. The argument of Mill's *On Liberty* is that it has good consequences for us to have such principles in support of the freedoms defended in that book. I have earlier suggested that a general principle of respect for persons also has a strong consequentialist justification.

Discussion of moral principles should not become mock-legalistic and casuistical at the expense of realising their psychological import-ance. Moral principles most matter, finally, in the shaping and artic-ulating of the person one wants to become. The final stages of ethical education should promote awareness that to a large extent we choose the people we are to be, and that it is better (more satisfactory in one's own experience, and more useful for others) to become a person of character rather than someone who is so highly flexible as to lack what is required for psychic integration. The ideal of ethical education is to be someone who naturally does what is right. But all, or almost all, of us are some distance from that goal. Confucius was a philosopher who paid unusually close attention to the conditions and stages of ethical development. Late in life, in reporting the stages of his own ethical progress, he ends by saying, 'At seventy I could follow the desires of my heart without transgressing the right.' This is a useful reminder that ethical education can take place during most or all of one's life.

NOTES AND REFERENCES

The quotations from Plato's *Republic* are from the Jowett translation, in *Dialogues of Plato* (New York, 1937), Vol. 1, pp. 623 and 877. I have discussed ethical education as education of character in 'Confucius and the problem of naturalness' (*Philosophy East and West*, 1968), and the role of moral rules in ethical education in 'Inhibition' (*Oxford Review of Education*, 1978). The essays of Lawrence Kohlberg referred to are 'Edu-cation for justice: a modern statement of the Platonic view', in Nancy F. and Theodore R. Sizer (eds), *Moral Education* (Cambridge, Mass., 1970), and 'The cognitive-developmental approach to moral education', in David Purpel and Kevin Ryan (eds), *Moral Education* (Berkeley, 1975). I quoted from p. 184 of the latter and p. 58 of the former. I also quoted from p. 484 of Carol Gilligan's 'In a different voice: women's conceptions of self and of morality' (*Harvard Educational Review*, 1977). An excellent general discussion of recent literature on moral education is to be found in Andrew Oldenquist's 'Moral education without moral education' (*Harvard Educational Review*, 1979). The quotation from Confucius is from the *Analects*, trans. W.E. Soothill, Book II, Chapter IV, p. 9.

Index

Adams, Robert Merrihew 111
Adkins, Arthur 52, 57
aesthetic condemnation 6ff, 12–13
aesthetic rules 23
animals 57, 63, 66, 99, 118
Aristotle 7, 12, 22, 25, 33, 59–60, 62, 71, 72, 83, 85, 86, 88, 89, 107, 109, 111, 143
attitude consequentialism 106ff
Aune, Bruce 32
autonomy 39–40, 41, 88, 108, 115

Bales, R. Eugene 141
Bennett, Jonathan 104, 111
Bentham, Jeremy 65, 66, 67, 95–6, 110, 111
Brandt, Richard 32, 71, 89
Brave New World 84, 115
Buddha 147
Buddhism 72, 142ff

Camus, Albert 141
Cassirer, Ernst 45
casuistry 21, 30, 59, 69, 113, 157, 159
categorical imperative 7–9, 16, 18–19, 32, 34, 36ff, 49, 55, 126
Chinese ethics 7
common sense 18, 19, 58ff, 98, 112–13, 116–17, 127–8, 133, 134, 139
Confucian philosophy 7, 12, 22, 60, 62–3, 143, 144
Confucius 62, 67, 111, 159
consequences 8, 16, 70, 72, 73–4, 93ff, 121ff, 143, 158
consequentialism 69, 70, 73–4, 79, 80–1, 82, 93ff, 145, 147, 148–9, 155, 159
Conze, Edward 149

divorce 38, 44
Donagan, Alan 19–20, 32, 69, 141
duty 7–9, 11
Dworkin, Ronald 33

equal consideration 40ff
'ethics' 12–13, 17
'expediency' 16, 110

Feinberg, Joel 101, 110
Fingarette, Herbert 111

Fitzhugh, George 65, 67
Foot, Philippa 17

Gauguin 38–9, 42, 44, 61, 69
Genovese, Eugene 65, 67
Gilligan, Carol 157, 159
Glover, Jonathan, 40, 46, 98, 110, 119, 120
Goodman, Nelson 57

Hammond, J. H. 65
happiness 16, 56, 57, 61, 66, 70, 75, 79–80, 94
Hare, R. M. 6–7, 33, 34–6, 89, 98, 126, 129, 155
Hart, H. L. 30, 33
Haslett, D. W. 110
Hegel 126, 129
Hobbes 4, 5, 17, 24
Hume 35, 45, 63, 97, 98, 110

ideals 17, 26, 140, 143, 144, 146, 148, 149
'ineffectual' 6
inhibition 28, 102, 105, 106, 123, 133, 136, 141, 146, 156

Jesus 14, 146
Johnson, Samuel 157
justice 16

Kant 4, 7–9, 16, 18–19, 31, 32, 34, 36ff, 50, 51, 52, 53, 55, 57, 60–1, 64, 67, 69–70, 73, 111, 113, 116, 118, 122, 124, 126, 138–9, 155, 156
Kneale, William 33
Kohlberg, Lawrence 153–4, 156–7, 159
Kovesi, Julius 33
Kuhn, T. S. 57

law 4, 17, 18, 29–33, 34, 126–7
Leibniz 122
Lenin 4, 17
Lomasky, Loren 120

McDowell, John 60, 67
Mackie, J. L. 45
manners 6ff, 12
mean, the 22, 33, 107
Mencius 63–4, 67

Mill, John Stuart 3, 10–12, 13, 15, 16–17, 65, 66, 67, 71, 80, 81–4, 89, 97, 101, 103, 111, 159
Milton 7
Moore, G. E. 12, 25, 42, 53–4, 71–3, 76, 87, 88, 89, 123, 139, 141
'moral' 7ff, 137–8
'moralistic' 3
morality and harm 5–6, 10, 11, 14–15, 16, 38
morality and sex 5, 11

Nagel, Thomas 51–2, 57
Newson, Elizabeth 144, 149
Newton 95–6
Nietzsche 3, 12, 17, 53, 57
Nozick, Robert 146, 149

objectivity of knowledge 16, 17, 61, 67
Odyssey, The 84
Oedipus 85
Oldenquist, Andrew 41, 46, 98, 156, 159
On Liberty 10–11, 16–17, 66, 101, 109, 111, 159
'original sin' 4

Parfit, Derek 89
Paton, H. J. 32
Planck, Max 55, 57
Plato 12, 86, 87, 150–4, 157, 159
pleasure 16, 28, 61, 70, 79–80, 85, 114, 143
prescriptivity 6–7, 10–11, 12–13, 17, 31, 137–8, 140
Price, A. W. 109, 111
principles 8–9, 11–12, 16, 17, 18–19, 50, 55, 64, 65, 155, 156, 158–9
punishment 3, 10–12, 16–17, 77

Questions of King Milinda 89

Rawls, John 43, 46, 57, 95, 110

Renoir, Jean 99
rights 57, 95, 98, 101–4, 106–7, 109, 110, 146
rigorism 19ff, 32, 49, 69, 100, 107, 115
Ross, Sir David 110
Rousseau 39, 41, 45
rules 13–14, 17, 18ff, 55, 56, 58ff, 69, 70, 88, 94, 95, 97, 100–1, 104, 106–7, 109, 110, 113ff, 133ff, 139, 153–6, 158, 159

Sartre 38, 45, 58, 61, 157
Satan 7
Schaff-Herzog Encyclopedia of Religious Knowledge 21
Scheffler, Israel 57
Searle, John 129
Sen, Amartya 89
Singer, Peter 66, 68, 119, 120
Smart, J. J. C. 67, 96
Socrates 80, 89, 151, 152
Sorin, Gerald 67
Strawson, P. F. 17, 54, 57
Sumner, L. W. 111, 120
'supererogatory' 14, 17, 66, 119, 140, 141, 142ff

Ten Commandments, the 4, 13, 29
Tolstoy 147
Troyat, Henri 149

universalisability 34–6, 98
Urmson, J. O. 17
utilitarianism 16, 40–1, 50, 51, 57, 60, 61, 65–6, 67, 69ff, 98, 112ff.

Voltaire 157

Walshe, W. H. 129
Warnock, G. L. 32
Wittgenstein 20, 32, 78
Wolff, Robert Paul 40, 45